Asking the right questions 2

TALKING WITH CLIENTS ABOUT
SEXUAL ORIENTATION
AND GENDER IDENTITY
IN MENTAL HEALTH, COUNSELLING
AND ADDICTION SETTINGS

First edition written by
Angela M. Barbara, Gloria Chaim and Farzana Doctor

Revised by
Angela M. Barbara and Farzana Doctor

Research co-ordinated and conducted by
Angela M. Barbara

camh

Centre for Addiction and Mental Health
Centre de toxicomanie et de santé mentale

A Pan American Health Organization / World Health Organization Collaborating Centre

National Library of Canada Cataloguing in Publication

Barbara, Angela M.

Asking the right questions, 2 : talking about sexual orientation and gender identity in mental health, counselling, and addiction settings /

Angela M. Barbara, Farzana Doctor, Gloria Chaim.

Includes bibliographical references.

ISBN – 978-0-88868-469-1 (PRINT)
ISBN – 978-0-88868-541-4 (PDF)
ISBN – 978-0-88868-542-1 (HTML)

1. Sexual orientation. 2. Gender identity. 3. Mental health services.
4. Counseling. 5. Addicts—Counseling of.
I. Doctor, Farzana II. Chaim, Gloria, 1955-
III. Centre for Addiction and Mental Health IV. Title.

HQ1075.B356 2004   362.2'04256'0866   C2004-901068-9

Printed in Canada

For information on other CAMH publications or to place an order, please contact:

Publication Services

Tel.: 1 800 661-1111 or 416 595-6059 in Toronto
E-mail: publications@camh.net

Website: www.camh.net

This manual was produced by the following:

Development: Julia Greenbaum, CAMH

Editorial: Sue McCluskey, CAMH

Design: Mara Korkola, CAMH

Print production: Christine Harris, CAMH

Marketing: Rosalicia Rondon, CAMH

2906/03-07 P167

Acknowledgments

The authors would like to acknowledge the following people whose input contributed to production of the original manual (*Asking the Right Questions*):

Toronto area

Christopher Hadden	John Gaylord
Jocelyn Urban	Adrienne Blenman
David Snoddy	Peter Sheridan
Lynne Green	Lyndsey Davies
Cherie Miller	Nelson Parker
Sharon McLeod	Anu Goodman
Dale Kuehl	Charlie Penzes
Meg Gibson	Isabela Herrmann
Craig Hamilton	Joanne Short
Mair Ellis	Joyce Conaty
Linda Cartain	Tammy Purdy
Anne Shaddick	Henry Seo
Helen Mcilroy	Jerry Schwalb
Greg Garrison	Rupert Raj
Susan Gapka	Amie Parikh

London area

Rev. Marcie Wexler	Richard Hudler
Scott Turton	Dr. Cecilia Preyra
Stephanie Howard	Derek Scott

Hamilton area

Dr. Andrew Gotowiec

Ottawa area

Isabelle Arpin

The authors would like to acknowledge the following people whose input contributed to production of the revised manual (*Asking the Right Questions 2*):

Toronto area

Nelson Parker	Terry McPhee
Valerie Gibson	Kyle Scanlon
Michele Clarke	Karyn Baker
Donna Akman	Dale Kuehl
Rupert Raj	Carole Baker
Hershel Tziporah Russell	

London area

Chris Williams	Mark Heathfield
Mary Jane Millar	Deb Selwyn
Cindy Smythe	Kim Trembly
Andrew Kicks	Mike Goulet
Cathy Cough	

Sudbury area

Kathryn Irwin-Seguin	Diane Sigouin
Angie DeMarco	

Vancouver area and B.C.

Louise Chivers	Jessie Bowen

Ottawa area

Ernie Gibbs

Sault Ste. Marie area

Nicole Hicks	Marc Bovine
Tammy Pajuluoma	

The authors would also like to acknowledge our community partners who participated in the production of the revised manual (*Asking the Right Questions 2*):

Toronto area
Sherbourne Health Centre
519 Community Centre
David Kelley Lesbian, Gay and HIV/AIDS Counselling Program, Family
    Service Association

London area
Canadian Mental Health Association
HALO Community Centre

Sudbury area
Northern Regional Recovery Continuum
Lakeside Centre

Ottawa area
Centretown Community Health Centre

Contents

1   Introduction
1   Why is this manual important?
2   Findings from two phases of the ARQ project—
            general conclusions
4   Using the manual
4   What is in this manual?
4   Using the ARQ2 guide
5   Using the background information
6   ARQ2 guide
8   Background information: Part A
9   A1: Significant relationships
10   A2: Sexual orientation
12   A3: Gender identity
14   A4: Relationship between sexual orientation/gender identity
            and substance use and/or mental health concerns
16 Background information: Part B
18   B1: Discrimination—homophobia, biphobia, transphobia
21   B2: Coming out and transitioning
24   B3: Openness about sexual orientation/gender identity
26   B4: Family issues
29   B5: Involvement in the community
31   B6: Body image and aging
34   B7: HIV concerns
36   B8: Relationship between substance use and/or mental
            health concerns and Part B items
38 Counsellor competence
48 Resources
48   Internet sites
51   Bibliography
55   Glossary
62 References
63 Appendix: Creating the guide and manual

Introduction

This manual is a revision of *Asking the Right Questions: Talking about Sexual Orientation and Gender Identity during Assessment for Drug and Alcohol Concerns.* We have expanded on the earlier version to include mental health issues in the assessment questions.

Substance use and mental health concerns may be related to sexual orientation and/or gender identity issues, particularly those issues relating to societal oppression—to provide effective treatment, therapists and counsellors must know about these issues.

This manual will help therapists/counsellors create an environment where lesbian, gay, bisexual, transgendered, transsexual, two-spirit, intersex, and queer (LGBTTTIQ) clients feel comfortable identifying themselves as such. This will allow therapists/counsellors to:
· best assess the specific needs of LGBTTTIQ clients
· engage these clients in a positive treatment process
· develop specifically tailored treatment plans
· make appropriate referrals.

WHY IS THIS MANUAL IMPORTANT?

Many clients are not open about their sexual orientation or gender identity in mainstream treatment/counselling facilities. They may feel uncomfortable or anxious, fearing negative responses or prejudiced attitudes from staff and other clients.

THIS MANUAL IS FOR ALL THERAPISTS, COUNSELLORS, OTHER CLINICIANS, NURSES AND DOCTORS ASSESSING OR TREATING CLIENTS WHO HAVE SUBSTANCE USE AND/OR MENTAL HEALTH CONCERNS.

LGBTTTIQ is a common acronym for lesbian, gay, bisexual, transsexual, transgendered, two-spirit, intersex and queer individuals/communities. This acronym may or may not be used in a particular community. For example, in some places, the acronym LGBT (for lesbian, gay, bisexual and transgendered/transsexual) may be more common. We have included this longer acronym to be more inclusive of the diversity within these communities.

A **SIGNIFICANT OTHER** is a life partner, domestic partner, lover, boyfriend, or girlfriend. It is often equivalent to the term "spouse" for LGBTTTIQ people.

SEXUAL MINORITIES include people who identify as LGBTTTIQ.

A **GAY** boy/man is someone whose primary sexual orientation is toward other boys/men.

A **LESBIAN** is a girl/woman whose primary sexual orientation is toward other girls/women.

A **BISEXUAL** person is someone whose sexual orientation is toward men and women.

A **TRANSGENDERED** person is someone who does not conform to society's gender norms of masculine/feminine.

A **TRANSSEXUAL** is a person who has an intense and sometimes long-term experience of being the sex opposite to his or her birth-assigned sex. Specifically, a **FEMALE-TO-MALE TRANSSEXUAL (TRANSMAN)** is assigned a female sex at birth, but feels like a male and identifies as a (transsexual) boy/man. A **MALE-TO-FEMALE TRANSSEXUAL (TRANSWOMAN)** is assigned a male sex at birth, but feels like a female and identifies as a (transsexual) girl/woman.

TRANS and **TRANSPEOPLE** are non-clinical terms that usually include transsexual, transgendered and other gender-variant people.

TWO-SPIRIT is an English word used by First Nation and other indigenous peoples for those in their cultures who are gay or lesbian, are intersex, transsexual, trans-gendered or have multiple gender identities.

INTERSEX is the term that has recently replaced "hermaphrodite." Intersex people possess some blend of male and female physical sex characteristics (see also www.isna.org).

QUEER is a term that has traditionally been used as a derogatory and offensive word for LGBTTTIQ people. Many have reclaimed this word and use it proudly to describe their identity.

Many clinicians are understanding of sexual orientation and gender identity issues. However, these clinicians may lack a repertoire of appropriate questions to ask about sexual orientation or gender identity, or they may be unaware of why such questions are necessary for clients of substance use and/or mental health services.

Some questions in standard assessments may be upsetting. For example, if a question about "significant others" is phrased in terms of opposite gender, an LGBTTTIQ person may feel uncomfortable.

Traditional assessment items/scales may not be accurate for all clients if the interpretations do not address the specific needs of different sexual orientations or gender identities.

Standard assessment instruments, such as provincially or state-mandated assessment tools, should be supplemented with population-specific questions to better assess the needs of LGBTTTIQ clients and formulate treatment/counselling plans.

FINDINGS FROM TWO PHASES OF THE ARQ PROJECT—
GENERAL CONCLUSIONS

The Centre for Addiction and Mental Health conducted a research project through its Rainbow Services (formerly known as LesBiGay Service), asking service providers and clients what should go into the original manual, which focused on substance use—this phase became known as ARQ (*Asking the Right Questions*). Further research was conducted to revise and expand the manual to also include mental health issues— this phase became known as ARQ2 (see the Appendix for a detailed description of each phase). Here are the general conclusions of the two phases of the project:

Therapists/counsellors should use sensitive and direct questions at assessment to determine the sexual orientation and gender identity of all clients.

LGBTTTIQ people have specific life factors that relate to substance use and/or mental health problems. These factors include:
· the "coming out" process
· gender transition
· societal oppression (e.g., homophobia, biphobia, transphobia)
· threats to socioeconomic security (e.g., housing, employment) because of discrimination
· internalized oppression
· loss of family support

- isolation and alienation
- the predominance of bars in LGBTTTIQ communities
- body image
- "passing"
- concerns with aging
- the impact of HIV and AIDS.

Awareness of clients' sexual orientation and gender identity is very relevant in effective treatment and counselling. However, many clients are not open about their sexual orientation or gender identity in mainstream treatment facilities—they may be uncomfortable, feeling anxious or afraid of negative responses or homophobic/biphobic/transphobic attitudes of staff and other clients.

Several factors contribute to client self-disclosure:
- feelings of safety
- non-judgmental and non-heterosexist/genderist attitudes of staff and other clients
- advertising of a service in LGBTTTIQ publications and communities
- LGBTTTIQ-positive stickers and posters
- use of non-biased, inclusive language
- confidentiality
- staff who are knowledgeable of LGBTTTIQ-specific issues.

The following factors enhance the experience of services for LGBTTTIQ people:
- availability of specialized programs/services
- composition of treatment/counselling groups based on sexual orientation and gender identity
- anti-discrimination policies
- LGBTTTIQ-positive materials in waiting areas
- access to LGBTTTIQ-positive therapists/counsellors.

Specialized addiction treatment programs and mental health counselling services are helpful and clinically relevant for LGBTTTIQ people. However, therapists/counsellors should not assume that LGBTTTIQ clients must be seen in specialized settings. Clients may prefer an LGBTTTIQ-specific program, if available, but they may also prefer mainstream services (e.g., general treatment programs) or other specialized services based on other aspects of their identity (e.g., aboriginal services, older person's services, women's services). At the Centre for Addiction and Mental Health (CAMH), we support the need for LGBTTTIQ-specialized services while making efforts to build capacity in mainstream services.

SEXUAL ORIENTATION is how someone thinks of oneself in terms of one's emotional, romantic or sexual attraction, desire or affection for another person.

GENDERISM is the assumption that all people must conform to society's gender norms and, specifically, the binary construct of only two genders (male and female). Genderism does not include or allow for people to be intersex, transgendered, transsexual, or genderqueer (see pages 12 to 13 for a discussion of gender).

Using the Manual

WHAT IS IN THIS MANUAL?

This manual includes
· the ARQ2 guide to be used with a standard substance use, mental health, or other service assessment (pages 6–7)
· background information to help therapists, counsellors, nurses, doctors, and other clinicians use the ARQ2 guide (pages 8–37)
· answers to common questions from counsellors (pages 38–47)
· a list of resources for counsellors (pages 48–54)
· a glossary of concepts, used throughout this manual, to help therapists/ counsellors familiarize themselves with terms that may be used by LGBTTTIQ clients and communities (pages 55–61).

USING THE ARQ2 GUIDE

There are two parts to the ARQ2 guide.

Part A is a one-page assessment form to be completed by the client, in the presence of the therapist/counsellor, during the initial assessment interview or early in the counselling process. It is used to identify clients' sexual orientation and gender identity and to ask about related concerns.

Part B is a set of eight open-ended interview items to be asked by the therapist/counsellor during assessment or early in the counselling/treatment process. It is used to identify LGBTTTIQ clients' concerns that will be relevant to treatment/case planning.

USING THE BACKGROUND INFORMATION

For each item on the ARQ2 guide, this manual gives the following background information:

- **Relevance/intent:** This information describes why the item was included in the guide. Understanding the intent can help you effectively phrase the items in Part B, and will help you respond if clients ask about the relevance of some of the questions.

- **Additional probes (Part B only):** This section contains suggested probes that you may want to use after each question. A probe is a question or prompt that is not in the ARQ2 guide itself, but that may give information to help you understand the client's responses more fully. We have not included a comprehensive list of probes. Each therapist/ counsellor has a personal style and will tailor probes to the particular client.

- **Client perceptions:** We have included quotations in this manual to give a fuller picture of the experiences and concerns of the clients who participated in the focus groups and interviews.

- **Therapist/counsellor perceptions:** The expertise of the therapists/ counsellors who contributed to this project is also depicted through quotations revealing their clinical knowledge with LGBTTTIQ clients and their experiences using the template or first version of this guide.

The ARQ2 Guide

PART A

TO BE COMPLETED BY CLIENT DURING ASSESSMENT INTERVIEW OR EARLY IN COUNSELLING

In our goal to match clients with the appropriate services, we ask these questions to better understand your needs. Please check all that apply.

1. Are you currently dating, sexually active or in a relationship(s)? ☐ yes ☐ no

   If yes... is (are) your partner(s) ☐ female ☐ male ☐ intersex ☐ transsexual ☐ transgendered

   ☐ two-spirit ☐ other? _____ ☐ prefer not to answer

   How long have you been together or dating? _____

   How important/significant is this (are these) relationship(s) to you? ☐ not much ☐ somewhat ☐ very much

   If you have had previous relationships, was (were) your partner(s) ☐ female ☐ male ☐ intersex

   ☐ transsexual ☐ transgendered ☐ two-spirit ☐ other? _____ ☐ prefer not to answer

2. How would you identify your sexual orientation?

   ☐ straight/heterosexual ☐ lesbian ☐ gay ☐ WSW (woman who has sex with women)

   ☐ bisexual ☐ MSM (man who has sex with men) ☐ queer

   ☐ transensual (person attracted to transsexual or transgendered people)

   ☐ polysexual ☐ two-spirit ☐ questioning ☐ asexual ☐ autosexual

   ☐ unsure ☐ other_____ ☐ prefer not to answer

   Do you have concerns related to your sexual orientation, or do you ever feel awkward about your sexual orientation?
   ☐ not at all ☐ a little ☐ somewhat ☐ a lot ☐ unsure ☐ prefer not to answer

3. How would you identify your gender identity?

   ☐ female ☐ male ☐ transsexual ☐ transgendered ☐ genderqueer

   ☐ two-spirit ☐ FTM (female-to-male) ☐ MTF (male-to-female) ☐ intersex

   ☐ unsure ☐ questioning ☐ other _____ ☐ prefer not to answer

   Do you have concerns related to your gender identity, or do you ever feel awkward about your gender identity?
   ☐ not at all ☐ a little ☐ somewhat ☐ a lot ☐ unsure ☐ prefer not to answer

4. Is your reason for getting help (substance use, mental health concerns) related to any issues around your sexual orientation or gender identity?

   ☐ not at all ☐ a little ☐ somewhat ☐ a lot ☐ unsure ☐ prefer not to answer

   Area for therapist comments:

The ARQ2 Guide

PART B
TO BE ADMINISTERED BY THERAPIST/COUNSELLOR
DURING ASSESSMENT INTERVIEW
OR EARLY IN COUNSELLING

1. Can you tell me about any particular problems you have faced because of discrimination based on your sexual orientation/gender identity?

2. At about what age did you first realize you were _____? What has it been like for you after coming out/transitioning to yourself and to others?

3. How open are you about your sexual orientation/gender identity? At work? At school? At home? With new acquaintances?

4. Tell me about your family. How has your sexual orientation/gender identity affected your relationship with your family? Do you have support from your family?

5. How are you involved in the lesbian, gay, bi, trans, two-spirit, intersex and/or queer (LGBTTTIQ) communities?

6. Do you have concerns about body image? Do you have concerns about aging? Do body image pressures and ageism in the lesbian, gay, bi, trans, two-spirit, intersex and/or queer (LGBTTTIQ) communities affect you?

7. HIV is a big concern for a lot of people. Can you tell me in what ways this may be true for you?

8. Do you use alcohol and/or other drugs to cope with any of the issues we mentioned? Are your mental health concerns related to any of the issues we mentioned?
   ☐ not at all   ☐ a little   ☐ somewhat   ☐ a lot

   If yes... in what ways?

Background Information

Part A

PART A IS TO BE ADMINISTERED WITH ALL CLIENTS AT THE ASSESSMENT INTERVIEW.

CLIENT PERCEPTIONS

"The therapist should ask, 'Are you currently in a relationship?' If the client says 'yes,' then ask: 'Is it heterosexual or homosexual?' It needs to be forthright. It should not seem like it is an issue. Don't ask what type of relationship it is. Then I would feel like I was being judged. Normalize it. Make it a matter-of-fact thing. They should also ask about identity, not just about relationships, since I could be in a relationship with a woman, but I am gay, which could be the reason for drinking. Someone asking me the question if I am gay would be the best thing that ever happened."

THERAPIST/COUNSELLOR PERCEPTIONS

"I ask. I am fairly direct. It is important to use language that is inclusive, i.e., 'partner, whether that be male or female.' No dancing around."

RELEVANCE/INTENT

The items are meant to invite clients to disclose information about their sexual orientation and gender identity. This helps you avoid making assumptions that may be inaccurate, and will help you identify LGBTTTIQ clients for whom Part B will be relevant.

Your comfort level with these questions will affect the comfort level of the client. Ask the questions in a matter-of-fact, straightforward manner, as you would any other question.

It is important to convey acceptance and openness to the client's responses.

At CAMH, Part A is offered to the clients to self-administer, with an introduction given by the therapist/counsellor about why it is used. For example, "We would like you to complete this form so we can better understand your situation," "We recognize that there is a variety of sexual orientations and gender identities, so we would like to ask the following questions," and "We ask all clients to fill this out at assessment."

Therapists/counsellors should instruct the client to check off as many boxes as they want and that apply.

SIGNIFICANT RELATIONSHIPS

Are you currently dating, sexually active or in a relationship(s)? ☐ yes ☐ no

If yes… is (are) your partner(s) ☐ female ☐ male ☐ intersex ☐ transsexual ☐ transgendered ☐ two-spirit ☐ other? _____ ☐ prefer not to answer

How long have you been together or dating? _____

How important/significant is this (are these) relationship(s) to you? ☐ not much ☐ somewhat ☐ very much

If you have had previous relationships, was (were) your partner(s) ☐ female ☐ male ☐ intersex ☐ transsexual ☐ transgendered ☐ two-spirit ☐ other? _____ ☐ prefer not to answer

RELEVANCE/INTENT

Same-gender relationships do not receive the same validation that most heterosexual relationships receive in society. Therefore, clients may feel uncomfortable being open about their relationships or the gender of their partner. This item will convey to the client that the therapist/counsellor or agency acknowledges, identifies and validates same-gender relationships.

These questions acknowledge and validate transgendered, transsexual and intersex partners.

Gender variance and diversity is also stigmatized in our society. Clients who have transgendered, transsexual or intersex partners may feel more comfortable disclosing their partner's gender identity when asked respectfully and directly.

Significant relationships are not always congruent with sexual orientation or sexual behaviour. For example, a client may be in a heterosexual marriage but be involved in an extramarital same-sex relationship or a bisexual man may be in a monogamous same-gender relationship.

The questions also acknowledge and validate multiple and non-monogamous partnerships. These relationships too are stigmatized in our society. Questions should be asked in a manner and tone that does not privilege monogamy over polyamory, multiple partnerships or other relationship forms.

Although LGBTTTIQ people may have to deal with specific relationship factors (e.g., invisibility of same-gender or trans partners, non-acceptance of partners by family, lack of outlets for discussing relationship dynamics and dating), therapists/counsellors should acknowledge that LGBTTTIQ people also face many of the same relationship issues that non-LGBTTTIQ people face. These include issues such as domestic violence or partner abuse, grief over the death of a partner, relationship breakups, inter-personal problems and parenting.

THESE QUESTIONS ARE INTENDED TO IDENTIFY AND VALIDATE ALL RELATIONSHIPS.

CLIENT PERCEPTIONS

"When I went to [addiction treatment agency], the nurse asked me, 'What's the name of your husband?' I said, 'I don't have a husband.' 'Okay,' she asked, 'is it your boyfriend?' I said, 'I have a partner.' She said, 'What's his name?' When it comes to these questions, it's so uncomfortable. I don't make it a big deal myself. I just said, 'Her name is [name].' But then you can see their faces changing. Then you feel uncomfortable for the rest of the questions."

THERAPIST/COUNSELLOR PERCEPTIONS

"Therapists must make it clear to the clients that they are comfortable with same-sex couples. We need to be inclusive of clients who have or have had relationships with transgendered men and women."

"Our questions on relationships are non-gender specific: 'Is your partner male or female?' I have seen women's faces light up when I put that question to them. It tells them it's okay to be a lesbian here."

SEXUAL ORIENTATION

How would you identify your sexual orientation?

☐ straight/heterosexual ☐ lesbian ☐ gay
☐ WSW (woman who has sex with women) ☐ bisexual
☐ MSM (man who has sex with men) ☐ queer
☐ transensual (person attracted to transsexual or transgendered people)
☐ polysexual ☐ two-spirit ☐ questioning
☐ asexual ☐ autosexual ☐ unsure
☐ other _____ ☐ prefer not to answer

Do you have concerns related to your sexual orientation, or do you ever feel awkward about your sexual orientation?

☐ not at all ☐ a little ☐ somewhat ☐ a lot ☐ unsure ☐ prefer not to answer

SEXUAL ORIENTATION
SHOULD ALWAYS BE ASKED ABOUT
REGARDLESS OF RELATIONSHIP STATUS.

CLIENT PERCEPTIONS

"Although I think a person's sexual orientation is a small aspect of their being, it can be a very big part of their life and it can be a very big part of the therapy process, because that's how we learn about ourselves, through our relationships. And while you're in therapy, you're going to have relationships, and you're going to bring it into therapy. You can't go and see a psychiatrist and never tell them that you're gay if you're gay. There has to be that open exchange."

"On the demographics form, did it say choose all that I apply? I always identify as bisexual and queer. And I am married to a male. So that can be interesting in assessment and counselling situations."

RELEVANCE/INTENT

This item is meant to include the most common terms clients may use to identify their sexual orientation. The list is not exhaustive; clients may have other words to define their sexual orientation. This item also helps to identify clients who may be questioning or struggling with their sexual orientation. Clients may check more than one term.

Significant relationships (and sexual behaviour) are distinct from sexual orientation, and one does not necessarily or consistently predict the other. Sexual orientation should always be asked about regardless of relationship status. For example, someone may indicate being in relationships with only men, but may identify as bisexual, or someone is married to a person of the opposite gender but identifies as gay.

For some people, sexual orientation is continuous and fixed throughout their lives. For others, sexual orientation may be fluid and change over time.

There is a broad spectrum of sexual orientations. One way to think about sexual orientation is as a fluid continuum that ranges from exclusive same-gender attraction to exclusive opposite-gender attraction, with many points in between.

Exclusively Straight Heterosexual	Bisexual Polysexual	Exclusively Lesbian Gay

It is important to note that not everyone who identifies as the same sexual orientation will fit in the same place on the continuum. For example, one bisexual person may fit directly in the middle of the continuum, but another bisexual person may fit away from the middle and closer to one end of the continuum than to the other.

When people are exploring their sexual orientation, they may try to find where they fit along the continuum. Clinicians are invited to reflect on their own sexual orientation to increase awareness of feelings and biases of this issue. A clinician's own feelings and biases may help or inhibit discussion of sexual orientation with clients.

Sometimes, people from marginalized ethnocultural/racial communities may not identify as or use labels they associate with the predominantly white (and often racist) LGBTTTIQ communities. For example, a woman of colour may choose a different label, such as "woman loving women" instead of lesbian. However, this example may not apply to all women of colour.

THERAPIST/COUNSELLOR PERCEPTIONS

"Allow the client to identify as gay, straight, etc. Don't worry about using a question regarding sexual orientation with a client who is straight. Use a preamble such as: 'We recognize all walks of life and welcome them all....' Set it up for all clients to answer questions truthfully."

POLYSEXUALITY is an orientation that does not limit affection, romance or sexual attraction to any one gender or sex, and that recognizes more than just two genders.

Someone who identifies as **ASEXUAL** may not be sexually and/or romantically active, or not sexually and/or romantically attracted to other persons.

AUTOSEXUAL describes someone whose significant sexual involvement is with oneself or someone who prefers masturbation over partnered sex.

Sexual behaviour is distinct from sexual orientation. These concepts should not be used interchangeably. For this reason, we include the terms **MAN WHO HAS SEX WITH MEN** and **WOMAN WHO HAS SEX WITH WOMEN**.

A **TRANSSENSUAL** person has a primary sexual or romantic attraction to transgendered and/or transsexual people.

GENDER IDENTITY

How would you identify your gender identity?

☐ female ☐ male ☐ transsexual ☐ transgendered ☐ genderqueer ☐ two-spirit

☐ FTM (female-to-male) ☐ MTF (male-to-female) ☐ intersex ☐ unsure

☐ questioning ☐ other_____ ☐ prefer not to answer

Do you have concerns related to your gender identity, or do you ever feel awkward about your gender identity?

☐ not at all ☐ a little ☐ somewhat ☐ a lot ☐ unsure ☐ prefer not to answer

GENDER IDENTITY
IS DISTINCT FROM SEXUAL ORIENTATION.

CLIENT PERCEPTIONS

"Sometimes people have very specific ideas about who is gay and who is straight and what a real transsexual person is supposed to be in terms of their sexual orientation. That's a huge problem. I remember being told flat out that my being bisexual or queer-identified as a transman was unusual. And I said, 'Actually, that's not true. Tons of the guys in the FTM community are bi or queer or gay-identified.' And unless counsellors have this conversation with you, they won't find out."

"Everyone experiences being trans differently. Some people have more intense feelings and more dysphoric feelings, which means they're really at odds with their gender. Some people know exactly which way they are going."

"In the Native communities, the respect is there. It's not like in the white society, where they call me trash, freak and a few other names. Because whenever a Native person sees me, most of them will go out of their way for me because I am special. The two-spirit being is a higher being, and I am supposed to have a higher wisdom."

RELEVANCE/INTENT

This question encourages disclosure of and discussion about gender identity and related concerns. Traditional options for gender, such as "male or female," do not include people who are transgendered, transsexual, intersex and others. This item invites people to be open about their gender identity.

Gender identity is distinct from sexual orientation. Regardless of gender, a person may identify as heterosexual, gay, bisexual or any other sexual orientation.

If clients are confused about this question, explain that some people's biological sex does not fit with who they feel they are. For example, some people with male biology may feel themselves to be female.

There can be many genders other than male and female. One way to think about gender identity is as a fluid continuum that ranges from more masculine to more feminine:

Masculine	Androgynous (not obviously male or female) Gender variant Gender non-conforming	Feminine

Transgendered and transsexual people cover the entire range of the continuum, from very "butch" (masculine) to very feminine. For example, a transsexual woman may be as feminine as a biological woman. A transsexual gay male may be less masculine than a butch lesbian.

When people are exploring their gender identity, they may be deciding where they fit along this continuum. Others (e.g., someone who identifies as genderqueer) may reject the continuum and gender categories altogether.

Clinicians are invited to think about their own gender identity to become conscious of feelings and preconceived notions about this issue. A clinician's own feelings and biases may help or hinder talking about gender identity with clients.

Gender is sometimes expressed differently in different contexts because there may be social roles or experiences that force, pressure or encourage us to experience our genders in more or less fluid ways. For example, people may be expected to express their gender in a certain kind of way within a workplace and may express their gender differently at home.

Sometimes, people from ethnocultural/racial communities may identify their gender identity in other ways. For example, some male-to-female transgendered clients from other cultures may identify as "lady boys" or "she-males."

THERAPIST/COUNSELLOR PERCEPTIONS

"As a therapist, I don't want to make assumptions about how someone identifies their gender. People who are transsexual or on the transgender continuum probably feel pretty alienated by the assumptions."

GENDER IDENTITY, which does not always correspond to biological sex, is a person's self-image or belief about being female or male. For example, some people with male biology may feel themselves to be female.

GENDER ROLES are the arbitrary rules, assigned by society, that define what clothing, behaviours, thoughts, feelings, relationships, etc. are considered appropriate and inappropriate for members of each sex.

GENDER TRANSITION is the period during which transsexual persons begin changing their appearance and bodies to match their internal identity.

A3

A4

RELATIONSHIP BETWEEN SEXUAL ORIENTATION/GENDER IDENTITY
AND SUBSTANCE USE AND/OR MENTAL HEALTH
Is your reason for getting help (substance use, mental health concerns) related to any issues around your sexual orientation or gender identity?
☐ not at all ☐ a little ☐ somewhat ☐ a lot ☐ unsure ☐ prefer not to answer

LGBTTTIQ PEOPLE HAVE SPECIFIC LIFE FACTORS THAT RELATE TO SUBSTANCE USE AND MENTAL HEALTH.

RELEVANCE/INTENT

LGBTTTIQ people have specific life factors that relate to substance use and mental health.

Sexual orientation and gender identity are not inherently related to increased susceptibility to substance use problems or mental health problems. However, any stress, worry or uncertainty related to sexual orientation or gender identity may be related to a client's use of substances, self-harm or suicidal behaviour.

CLIENT PERCEPTIONS

"When it comes to the mental health system and trans people, the idea is that as soon as you've transitioned, you won't be depressed anymore. But if you transition and you are depressed, there is the fear that medical professionals will assume that transitioning was a bad thing and that you made a mistake. But I say that there's stigma in society as a result of being trans, as a result of not passing, as a result of being seen as a freak. Are we not supposed to experience that oppression? Are we somehow supposed to just let it fall off our shoulders and not be affected by it? Some doctors see this only as a medical transition issue. They don't understand at all the social implications of what we experience and how it affects us."

Stress, prejudice and discrimination related to sexual orientation or gender identity create a stressful social environment that can lead to mental health problems for LGBTTTIQ people (Meyer, 2003).

Historically, the psychiatric system has linked homosexuality and gender identity issues with mental illness, which may trouble clients. Clinicians must be careful not to pathologize, or imply a pathological connection between, clients' mental health/substance use concerns and their identity.

CLIENT PERCEPTIONS

"It's like you have to deal with two things instead of just one. You're dealing with a mental illness and you are struggling with your sexual orientation. It seems doubly hard."

THERAPIST/COUNSELLOR PERCEPTIONS

"Oppression is bad for people's health."

"How a client's identity is integrated affects other problems: depression, self-esteem, substance use."

A4

Background Information

Part B

PART B SHOULD BE CONSIDERED A GUIDE TO A CONVERSATION.

To be administered with clients who:
· identify as lesbian, gay, bisexual, two-spirit, MSM, WSW, queer, transsensual, polysexual, unsure or questioning
OR
· identify as transsexual, transgendered, FTM, MTF, genderqueer, or intersex.

CLIENT PERCEPTIONS

"In the assessment, it worked very well for me, because I realized that it wasn't just a question of sexuality, but that there might be certain issues for lesbians and gay people that impact on why we use substances or that could be different."

"If there was something I was holding back and I was uncertain of whether I could feel comfortable talking about it, the fact that the interviewer was going to address that issue would already make it a little more comfortable for me. I would start to think, 'Gee, maybe not today, but maybe next time, I can talk about this or something.' "

Part B may also be relevant for clients who:
· have a current or past relationship(s) with people of the same gender
· identify concerns, questioning, or awkwardness related to sexual orientation and/or gender identity.

We recommend that Part B be administered either at assessment by the person who will be counselling the client or, if another therapist/counsellor conducts the assessment, at the first or second meeting (early in the counselling/treatment process). However, Part B, or elements of it, can also be used at any point during therapy.

Part B is a set of interview questions to gather information about clients. **It should be considered a guide to a conversation.** The information you gather should be used in creating the treatment/counselling plan for clients. For example, if someone identifies difficulty with internalized oppression, you may want to ensure that the person's individual/group therapy includes ways to discuss and resolve these issues.

Clients are more open to answering questions if the questions are posed in a direct, non-confrontational manner. In some cases, you may simply read the question off the page, as written. In other cases, you may find it appropriate to paraphrase.

The items in Part B are meant to identify issues that LGBTTTIQ clients may be dealing with. The items are open-ended questions, to encourage clients to volunteer information they might not realize is important.

Some items may seem to overlap. It may not be necessary to ask every question. Asking all these questions, however, gives the client the chance to discuss all relevant issues.

The content of the items and the sensitivity of the therapist/counsellor are very important. The exact wording and order of the items are less important. Part B should be used as a guide, until you understand the unique issues that are faced by LGBTTTIQ clients with substance use and/or mental health problems.

Validate the concerns expressed by clients. Remember, clients who are marginalized face stress that is hurtful and sometimes traumatic.

THERAPIST/COUNSELLOR PERCEPTIONS

"Because they don't feel safe, [clients] never quite say, 'Yes, I am gay or lesbian.' And then they get tossed into the general group. And then I meet them four years later, saying, 'I went to this place or I went to that place, but it didn't work for me 'cause I never got to deal with my coming out.' Okay. 'Well maybe if you'd said that.' 'Okay, but they never asked.' "

B

B1

DISCRIMINATION—HOMOPHOBIA, BIPHOBIA, TRANSPHOBIA

Can you tell me about any particular problems you have faced because of discrimination based on your sexual orientation/gender identity?

DISCRIMINATION
HOMOPHOBIA BIPHOBIA TRANSPHOBIA

CLIENT PERCEPTIONS

"I was out to my friends and family but not at work. There were just so many homophobic jokes that went on at work. Plus, I would hear things at work that were offensive and I couldn't say anything. Then when I finished work after a long day, I would just treat the pain with some drugs. So, absolutely for me, homophobia was a big part of the drug issue. Not an excuse, but a factor."

"If you're alone with your drug, you don't experience the homophobia."

"I think that homophobia and biphobia are definitely relevant for people coming in for treatment for mental illness. Where it's really, really, really relevant is people staying well once you're well and sustaining a state of wellness, because homophobia is one of those things that will start you going downhill."

"It's okay to be gay. It's okay to be a lesbian. It's okay to be a drag queen. But if you're transgendered, you're the scum of the earth. It's a very, very, very rotten life. People that seem to be normal go berserk when they meet me. I am the ultimate challenge to everything. I am the ultimate challenge to religion. I am the ultimate challenge to the male/female role definition. I am the ultimate challenge to what society says I should be."

RELEVANCE/INTENT

If clients have had personal experiences of discrimination based on their sexual orientation or gender identity, these experiences may be related to substance use behaviour and/or mental health concerns.

It is difficult for LGBTTTIQ people not to be aware of and affected by negative social images of themselves.

Examples of discrimination include:
· bullying, verbal abuse, insults, harassment or name-calling
· rejection and social exclusion
· assault or bashing
· withholding services, jobs, housing or opportunities
· displaying discomfort or fear in the presence of LGBTTTIQ people.

Sexual orientation and gender identity are interconnected with many other identities, such as race, ethnicity, culture, religion, immigration status and language. Discrimination based on sexual orientation or gender identity cannot be separated from other forms of societal oppression, such as racism, sexism, classism and ableism.

Clients need to know that you recognize the context of societal oppression faced by LGBTTTIQ people. Clients may worry that service providers will not respect or understand their circumstances, will be ignorant about LGBTTTIQ issues or will pathologize their identity. Clients may also worry that counsellors will make stereotypical assumptions about the relationship between their sexual orientation or gender identity and their substance use or mental health problems.

Transsexual and transgendered clients who have difficulty "passing" as their identified gender are at much higher risk for discrimination. Passing helps trans clients get and keep jobs and housing, and avoid being the target of violence. Barriers, such as cost, to gender transition procedures (e.g., hormone therapy, electrolysis, surgery) can make it difficult to pass.

Other people who do not conform to this society's gender norms, such as feminine men, masculine women and androgynous people, also face higher levels of discrimination compared to those who do conform to societal gender norms.

Clinicians should consider the ways in which their own organization or practices maintain a discriminatory stance towards LGBTTTIQ people. Here is a list of some common examples:
· a transgendered and transsexual person who is denied hormones or surgery if he or she is seen to have mental health concerns
· a gay man in addiction treatment who is told to not be "distracted" by issues related to his identity
· a transwoman who is told she cannot use a women's lounge
· a staff person refusing to treat a LGBTTTIQ person because it is "against his religion"
· a clinician who exoticizes a bisexual client and asks about sexual practices when it is not relevant to treatment
· a clinician who encourages a butch lesbian to be more feminine
· a staff member who refuses a same-gender partner or other chosen family the right to visit a hospitalized loved one
· a lack of gender neutral washrooms.

For Internet resources on discrimination, please see the Resources section (page 50)

THERAPIST/COUNSELLOR PERCEPTIONS

"The LGBTTTIQ community is already marginalized. The mental health community is already marginalized. When you belong to two marginalized groups, you become that much further marginalized."

"My gay clients talk about how it's in your file now that you're different or you're gay. And then everyone is, like, 'Are you okay with that? With being gay?' My sense is that it's not so much being gay that's the problem in the first place, but what is the problem is homophobia or that clients are treated differently."

"It's a central issue. How can it not be? They are traumatized by discrimination, often on a daily, weekly, monthly, constant basis. That kind of repetitive trauma has probably been happening for a very long time."

PASSING refers to appearing and being accepted in the world as one's identified gender. Passing can also refer to hiding one's sexual orientation, as in "passing for straight."

B1

HETEROSEXISM is the assumption that all people are or should be heterosexual and that identifying as heterosexual and having sexual or romantic attractions only to members of the opposite sex is good and acceptable. If these assumptions are made unconsciously, they are called *default assumptions*. An example is asking a woman if she has a husband, which reinforces the invisibility that lesbian, gay and bisexual people experience.

Like other forms of discrimination, **HETEROSEXISM**, **HOMOPHOBIA**, **BIPHOBIA** and **TRANSPHOBIA** are often invisible and unnoticed to those who are not their targets.

HATE CRIMES are offences that are motivated by hatred against victims based on their actual or perceived race, color, religion, national origin, ethnicity, gender, disability or sexual orientation.

ADDITIONAL PROBES

What has it been like for you to be LGBTTTIQ?

Have you had any problems because of people's dislike of LGBTTTIQ people?

Have you had to deal with specific challenges in your life because of homophobia, biphobia and/or transphobia?

Have you had any problems because of discrimination at work, at school, in health care services, in social services?

COMING OUT AND TRANSITIONING
At about what age did you first realize you were _____?
What has it been like for you after coming out/transitioning to yourself and to others?

RELEVANCE/INTENT

COMING OUT
AND TRANSITIONING

The blank (_____) in this item (and throughout the remainder of this guide) should be filled in with the client's response to item A2 or A3 (e.g., lesbian, queer, transgendered). If you need clarity, ask clients how they would like their identity to be addressed (e.g., a female client may want to be called a dyke or a male-to-female transsexual may want to be called a transwoman).

Coming out is a significant process in the lives of LGBTTTIQ people. It is a process, not an either/or phenomenon—it is not enough to ask if the client is "out of the closet."

For transgendered and transsexual people, the coming-out process may also be referred to as a transitioning process.

Coming out or transitioning to certain people may result in social rejection, criticism, violence, disapproval, shock and the threat of non-confidentiality —these reactions can cause long-lasting harm to LGBTTTIQ people.

People may turn to or continue substance use to deal with the various emotions, reactions from family and peers, and social isolation that can accompany the coming-out or transitioning process. People may also use drugs and alcohol as a way to express or suppress same-sex desire or gender expression. For example, a woman may use cannabis to have sex with her husband to whom she is not attracted, or a woman may only have sex with another woman when drunk because of shame or guilt associated with internalized oppression. People can also experience increased levels of anxiety, depression and thoughts of suicide while working through the challenges of coming out or transitioning.

It is important to note that coming out and transitioning may also be a time of liberation, joy and excitement. For some people, mental health may vastly improve as they become "more of who they are."

CLIENT PERCEPTIONS

"When I came out, I actually stopped using drugs. I'm still going through the process."

"Coming out is a profound psychological transformation. You're basically redefining yourself in the eyes of everybody. It's a very deep, very intimate thing. It's tremendously important. It has to do with your self-perception as well as how other people see you."

"I think it de-stressed me a whole lot. Coming out, you can be yourself. And when you are keeping that secret from people and you are all worried that someone is going to figure it out and they are not going to accept you, that just increases the depression, increases the dissociation, increases all this stuff. But when you start learning that people are not going to hate you, I think it makes your self-esteem go up. Most people with mental health issues have some sort of a low self-esteem thing going down. And when people start accepting you for who you are, I mean my self-esteem went up."

CLIENT PERCEPTIONS

"When, I came out, it was loud. It was a really scary time, so I took the fear like the bull by the horns and said, 'Wow. It's scary, so let's just do it, really big, and then it will be over. I think I can muster some courage for a day, so let's do it all today. Everyone at school will know and my dad will know. Everyone I know will know. And I'll phone everyone I ever knew and tell them.' So it was just, 'Bang, here you go' and not at all sensitive to anyone on the receiving end. And then I was very outward at school and the response was not good at all. I got a lot of graffiti on my locker. I had a couple of really close friends so that was okay in that way. I got beaten up once in my locker bay just at the end of school, and I stopped going to school at that point. I was fifteen and I never finished high school."

THERAPIST/COUNSELLOR PERCEPTIONS

"Secrecy if not out. It makes people not feel good about themselves. They use escapism, such as drinking or using drugs, to obliterate their sorrows."

"Often clients come in here who are in the process of wondering whether they are going to come out as transmen, and grappling with that set of issues. Many, not all, but many, come from a lesbian background. And that experience of coming out as a lesbian and telling certain stories about oneself as a lesbian. And then for those who come out as trans, there is a kind of re-evaluation of all those narratives and a selection of other narratives."

It is a valid choice for LGBTTTIQ people to decide when and where they come out, as they weigh the consequences. For example, someone may be out at home but not at work, or vice versa. Young people dependent on parents or caregivers may choose to wait until they are independent, fearing being rejected or kicked out of the home.

Sometimes, clients who come out or transition later in life experience a "second adolescence" in which they must negotiate interpersonal relationships and their own feelings—tasks they may not have been able to do in a heterosexist environment when younger.

Therapists/counsellors can help clients work through coming-out/transitioning issues and develop positive identities as LGBTTTIQ.

To be an ally to a client who is coming out or transitioning, you can:
· provide information about coming out, to normalize the experience
· provide information about community resources
· pay attention both to the individual and to the social context; that is, if the client expresses fear about coming out at work, help the client identify his or her own feelings as well as provide information about societal homo/bi/transphobia and human rights in these areas.

Various coming-out models exist—these can help clinicians familiarize themselves with the experience. The Cass model for lesbians and gay men (Cass, 1979) consists of six stages:
· Identity confusion—people are unsure of who they are.
· Identity comparison—people identify that they are different from others.
· Identity tolerance—people believe they might be lesbian or gay and seek out a community.
· Identity acceptance—people identify as lesbian or gay and share this with some significant others.
· Identity pride—people further disclose their identity, embrace this new identity and immerse themselves in the gay or lesbian communities and culture.
· Identity synthesis—people fully integrate their identity into a larger picture of themselves, and their sexual orientation is no longer an issue.

The coming-out processes for bisexual people are distinct, yet there may be some similarities with Cass's stage model.

Another model, by Devor (1997), consists of 14 identity development stages for female-to-male transsexuals:

· Abiding anxiety—unfocused gender and sex discomfort.
· Identity confusion—first doubts about suitability of assigned gender and sex.
· Identity comparison—seeking and weighing alternative female identities.
· Discovery—learning that female-to-male transsexualism exists.
· Identity confusion—first doubts about the authenticity of own transsexualism.
· Identity comparison—testing transsexual identity using transsexual reference group.
· Identity tolerance—identity as probably transsexual.
· Delay—waiting for changed circumstances; looking for confirmation of transsexual identity.
· Identity acceptance—transsexual identity established.
· Delay—transsexual identity deepens; no longer identify as women and females.
· Transition—Changing genders, between sexes.
· Identity acceptance—identities established as transsexual men.
· Integration—transsexuality most visible.
· Identity pride—publicly transsexual.

ADDITIONAL PROBES

Whom did you tell? How did they handle it?

Did you go to bars when you came out?

Are there areas in your life where you feel you are not out?

Did you find that you used more alcohol or other drugs, or that your mental health was affected, during the coming-out/transitioning process?

THERAPIST/COUNSELLOR PERCEPTIONS

"When clients are trying to decide whether or not they're coming out, there are certain things that you need to ask them to help them around. Do you feel safe? Who are you living with and is that stable? It might be safer for them to stay in the closet for the next year until they're done college if they are getting full support from their parents. But, also looking at the other side, that the most unsafe for someone to be is in the closet, because their highest risk for suicide is while they're in the closet. So, it's that juggling act."

"It never stops too. I mean, once you come out, you're coming out the rest of your life."

COMING OUT is the process by which LGBTTTIQ people acknowledge and disclose their sexual orientation or gender identity to themselves and others.

TRANSITIONING is the process by which transsexual people change their appearance and body to match their internal (gender) identity, while living their lives full-time in their preferred gender role.

B2

OPENNESS ABOUT SEXUAL ORIENTATION/GENDER IDENTITY
How open are you about your sexual orientation/gender identity?
At work? At school? At home? With new acquaintances?

THIS ITEM HELPS DETERMINE A CLIENT'S
PUBLIC IDENTIFICATION AS LGBTTTIQ.

CLIENT PERCEPTIONS

"Coming to terms with my sexuality was an issue and it caused me to drink. As soon as I started drinking in high school, it was problem drinking from the very first time. And I think it was all because I was pretty miserable as a teenager with my secret."

"I'm still trying to deal with my own inner homophobia. If I were in a relationship, still, at this point in my life, I would not be comfortable to walk down the street holding hands with another guy. I would actually push somebody away from me for doing that. And that's just the way I feel inside."

"I work in a business where everybody is married, with children and a dog and a white picket fence. And a lot of times they ask me why I'm not married, and I struggle with that. I always say, 'Because I haven't found the right person,' but, meanwhile, I'll be in a relationship with a woman."

RELEVANCE/INTENT

This item helps determine a client's public identification as LGBTTTIQ and will also help determine the client's level of internalized oppression (i.e., internalized homophobia, internalized biphobia, internalized transphobia). When people grow up in a culture with widespread heterosexism and rigid attitudes about gender, it is hard to avoid internalizing these attitudes to some extent. One of the most important treatment/counselling issues for LGBTTTIQ clients is to resolve internalized oppression and shame related to sexual orientation or gender identity.

Other dimensions of internalized oppression include:
· discomfort or awkward personal feelings about being LGBTTTIQ
· lack of connection with LGBTTTIQ communities
· negative moral and religious attitudes toward LGBTTTIQ people
· negative attitudes toward other LGBTTTIQ people.

Therapists/counsellors should be careful to distinguish between internalized oppression and a legitimate fear of societal oppression (e.g., fearing being fired from a job or having one's immigration status compromised due to societal homophobia).

Therapists/counsellors must be careful to avoid colluding with clients' internalized oppression. Wherever possible, therapists/counsellors should help clients gain awareness by gently challenging expression of internalized oppression. For example, a client may say, "Lesbian relationships don't last. Lesbians are so messed up." A therapist/counsellor can challenge this by asking, "Is that true for all lesbians?" and by pointing out exceptions, "I know of many lesbians who are in positive relationships."

Therapists/counsellors may have a role to play in encouraging clients to challenge societal oppression by becoming involved in individual or group activism. Becoming involved in community groups and actively confronting homo/bi/transphobia can be helpful for some clients.

ADDITIONAL PROBES

Do you want others to be aware of your sexual orientation/gender identity?

Are you worried about others finding out about your sexual orientation/gender identity?

How do you feel about being an out _____?

Are others aware that you have a same-sex/trans partner?

Do others know about your gender transition?

B3

B4

Tell me about your family. How has your sexual orientation/gender identity affected your relationship with your family? Do you have support from your family?

THIS ITEM ASSESSES THE CLIENT'S RELATIONSHIP TO FAMILY OF ORIGIN AND FAMILY OF CHOICE, AND DETERMINES THE LEVEL OF SUPPORT.

CLIENT PERCEPTIONS

"I came out to my mother and that's when my drinking went out of control."

"We're never going to be able to have children. If you don't have money, you can't do in vitro fertilization. If you have a mental illness, it's hard to adopt. It's even harder for us to adopt because we are a lesbian couple and we each have been diagnosed with mental illness. So, we're dealing with that when we both really want children."

RELEVANCE/INTENT

This item assesses the client's relationship to family of origin and family of choice, and determines the level of support.

Issues surrounding the traditional family or family of origin have a different theme and impact for LGBTTTIQ people than for those who are non-LGBTTTIQ.

When disclosing their sexual orientation or gender identity, LGBTTTIQ people may fear the reaction of parents, friends, children and extended family. To maintain a positive and supportive relationship with family members, some LGBTTTIQ people choose non-disclosure. Others who choose to come out do not always receive support from their family during or after coming out.

Same-gender partners or trans partners may not be included into the family or treated the same way that non-LGBTTTIQ partners are. For example, a straight woman's husband is regarded as a son by her parents, whereas a lesbian's female partner is regarded as "only a friend" or "roommate" by her parents.

People who have faced familial rejection may have different support systems or "chosen" families, made up of friends and past or current partners and lovers. For people of colour, family can represent a shelter from racism. If LGBTTTIQ people of colour experience lack of support or discrimination at home, it can be particularly isolating for them. They may also need to create a chosen family, which includes people from their own marginalized communities. Counsellors/therapists should always validate clients' chosen families.

For some LGBTTTIQ clients, sexual/romantic relationships are not always the most significant ones in their lives. For example, someone may be emotionally closer to a biological sibling or a chosen family member than to any short- or long-term lovers.

LGBTTTIQ people may also create families of their own by becoming parents—this should be acknowledged by clinicians. LGBTTTIQ parents often face struggles in choosing how/when/if to come out to their children. The children also face societal discrimination, and the parents sometimes have to help them cope with this.

Some people may be unable to form other social contacts and support systems once they have been alienated from their families.

In spite of support systems they may have, some LGBTTTIQ people may use substances or other harmful coping strategies (e.g., problematic eating, overspending, self-harm) to cope with the pain of rejection, isolation or conflict related to their sexual orientation or gender identity.

For Internet resources on family issues, please see the Resources section (page 50).

CLIENT PERCEPTIONS

"My daughter has a rough time in high school. She goes to Pride every year with me and if she wears her Pride T-shirt to school, other students are nasty and cruel. She has short hair and they say, 'Well, I guess you're going to be like your mom,' even though she's not gay. And if she is, so what? I'm going to be proud of her no matter what. My kids put up with more than I have sometimes."

THERAPIST/COUNSELLOR PERCEPTIONS

"When you add a mental health issue on top, you have twice the risk of not only hassle, but being disowned from the family. Some families are not exactly supportive of mental health issues either. So then you've got a double whammy."

"Trans people have a difficult time with their families, because they are trying to get acceptance from their families. And in some cases, for example, a transwoman's family members are not able to make the shift right away to using the correct pronoun. So they have these ongoing struggles to get family members to acknowledge who they are and to use the correct words to refer to them."

B4

THERAPIST/COUNSELLOR PERCEPTIONS

"If you have been part of a certain family unit or an extended family unit and suddenly you lose that, it takes a long time to rebuild. It isn't easy, especially if you are just coming out and just beginning to familiarize yourself with the culture. It can be scary."

"Some people, if their parents are very religious or from different cultures, they don't tell the parents. They just can't go there. They're struggling with those cultural familial constraints."

FAMILY OF ORIGIN is the biological family or the family that was significant in a person's early development.

FAMILY OF CHOICE or **CHOSEN FAMILY** refers to the people who provide support, nurturing and acceptance and are significant to a person.

ADDITIONAL PROBES

Who are the members of your family?

Are you out to your mother, father, brother(s), sister(s), children, family members?

What did your family do when you came out?

What are your concerns about coming out to your family?

Are you still part of the family? Are you welcome in the family?

What is your relationship like with your family?

Does your family welcome your partner(s)?

Do you have children? Have you come out to your children? What has that been like for you and for them?

If you are isolated from your family of origin, do you have a chosen family?

INVOLVEMENT IN THE COMMUNITY

How are you involved in the lesbian, gay, bi, trans, two-spirit, intersex and/or queer (LGBTTTIQ) communities?

RELEVANCE/INTENT

THE DEGREE TO WHICH A PERSON IDENTIFIES WITH A COMMUNITY IS A MAJOR RESILIENCY FACTOR.

This item assesses the client's connection to LGBTTTIQ communities and social supports (or lack of), to find if social isolation is an issue for the client. This item can also help determine the client's level of internalized oppression (e.g., internalized homophobia).

The degree to which a person identifies with a community is a major resiliency factor. Facing discrimination—from families and society—causes many LGBTTTIQ people to turn to their own communities for support.

What's more, some LGBTTTIQ people face double or triple marginalization (e.g., those with physical disabilities), which makes it even harder to find support. Many LGBTTTIQ people of colour may find themselves in predominately white, middle-class LGBTTTIQ communities. Rural LGBTTTIQ clients may have greater problems finding a community, and sometimes when they do find one, that community may be predominantly urban.

A strong social support network is key to recovering from substance use and/or mental health problems. The gay/lesbian bar has traditionally been a social centre of LGBTTTIQ communities, offering an environment where people can meet and socialize and be safe from societal prejudice. Until recently, there were few social alternatives to the bar, rave or circuit party scenes that allowed LGBTTTIQ people to go out, relax and feel part of the community. Therapists/counsellors should determine if the client relies primarily on bars or clubs for socializing, as there is often a tremendous presence of alcohol and various other substances in these spaces.

In some small communities, there are no ways to socialize with other LGBTTTIQ people. People in such communities might benefit from the Internet's resources.

CLIENT PERCEPTIONS

"I think gay people grow up believing, 'I don't belong. I'm a misfit. I wouldn't be welcome there.' It goes back to our social options being limited. If you're straight, you can go anywhere and do anything. If you're openly gay, you're restricted in terms of where you can go and feel comfortable. And for a lot of people who don't want to spend lots of time in bars or who have a lot of internalized homophobia and maybe find the social scenes uncomfortable, cutting ourselves off is sometimes the option. I think there's probably a tremendous amount of loneliness in the gay community."

"What is there in the gay community besides the bar scene?"

"I have hardly any friends and I have no ties to the gay community. I'm still trying to accept that I may be bisexual or gay, and when I come to terms with it, maybe I will make some connections."

THERAPIST/COUNSELLOR PERCEPTIONS

"I suspect in the gay and lesbian community there's two closets: one closet for mental health and one closet for being gay. In a large hospital it's better to play you're straight. So you're in the closet about being gay. But in the gay community, if you have major mental health issues, it's better to pretend that you're not depressed or you're not bipolar."

ADDITIONAL PROBES

(Note: the blank _____ in the following probes should be filled in with the client's response to item A2 or A3, e.g., gay, bisexual, transsexual.)

Do you have _____ friends?

Do you go to or attend any _____ groups or events?

In what ways have you explored the _____ communities?

How comfortable do you feel in social situations involving other _____ (people)?

Do you feel isolated or separate from other _____ (people)?

Are you familiar with community resources for _____, such as organizations, sports teams, bookstores, bars, groups, festivals, etc.?

BODY IMAGE AND AGING
Do you have concerns about body image? Do you have concerns about aging? Do body image pressures and ageism in the lesbian, gay, bi, trans, two-spirit, intersex and/or queer (LGBTTTIQ) communities affect you?

RELEVANCE/INTENT

BODY IMAGE, APPEARANCE, YOUTH AND FASHION CAN BE IMPORTANT ISSUES FOR ALL LGBTTTIQ PEOPLE.

Body image, appearance, youth and fashion can be important issues for all LGBTTTIQ people. Male gay culture places great emphasis on a lean and muscular body ideal, youth, appearance and fashion. Stereotypes of male beauty contribute to low self-esteem and alienation of gay and bisexual men who do not fit these images. These factors increase the risk for eating disorders, depression, low self-esteem and isolation.

Stereotypes of beauty, self-esteem and appearance are also an important issue for lesbians and bisexual women. Although lesbian culture may be more tolerant of diverse body sizes and shapes, women have been exposed since childhood to media and societal messages that promote thinness and attractiveness. This makes body image a relevant topic for lesbians and bisexual women.

Transgendered, intersex and transsexual people often have a difficult relationship with their bodies, given that their gender identity doesn't necessarily match up with their biological sex. Some transsexual people experience a great deal of discomfort with differences between the way they look and the way they want to look. For example, a male-to-female transsexual woman may feel too masculine and wish to be more feminine. This discomfort can contribute to loss of self-esteem.

CLIENT PERCEPTIONS

"You've got to be 20-something. You've got to have a skinny waist. You've got to have big muscles. Your penis has to be a certain length. And you've got to be young.... You look at any of the gay media and it's all young, skinny, drop-dead-gorgeous guys. And these images, as tasty as they might look, are absolutely impossible to live up to. I think the gay community suffers from that in the same way that women do. There's just a profound pressure to conform to culture stereotype."

"The gay community is very cruel in its treatment of anyone who is over the age of 23 as far as I'm concerned. You have to be between 14 and 18 to be loved, admired and wanted. Over 18 and you are finished."

CLIENT PERCEPTIONS

"The social scene is almost off-limits to a lot of people with mental illness, because the bar scene is very much a scene of aesthetics. It's all about how you look. When you're mentally ill, maybe you have less money. Your clothes aren't quite as snazzy. You might be on medication that makes you heavy and has a whole sedative effect on your body. There are economic factors within that community, particularly with women and transpeople that makes it harder to have the cutest clothes or whatever is hot this week. Certainly because of the weight that people put on with medication, or the lethargy, it's harder to go into that environment and feel comfortable because it's so all about how you look. So you get pushed out of that scene, because it's just not a comfortable place to be. It's just one more place you can't go."

Although not all transpeople have a desire to pass, some may also become preoccupied with passing successfully as the gender they set out to present. Passing can be made more difficult because of restrictive gender expectations (e.g., men must be muscular). Difficulty in passing makes someone susceptible to harassment or abuse and can lead to depression, anxiety, despair and substance use.

Body image and physical appearance may also be more of a problem for clients with visible physical disabilities or for those from other marginalized communities who do not fit into dominant "standards" of beauty.

Older people face a lack of visibility within mainstream and LGBTTTIQ communities alike. Our society places a higher value on youth and tends to assume that older people are non-sexual.

However, older LGBTTTIQ people have begun to create a presence for themselves, meeting to create supportive networks and services. In Toronto, Ontario, the 519 Church Street Community Centre provides a resource centre for LGBTTTIQ people. This centre conducted a needs assessment that revealed the need for sweeping changes to services for older adults, including LGBTTTIQ-positive housing, geriatric care and social activities. The report also suggested changes to LGBTTTIQ organizations, such as including older people in leadership roles, advocacy efforts and a "cultural shift" in the way that the community views, recognizes and celebrates it elders (Harmer, 2000).

ADDITIONAL PROBES

Have you ever worried about getting older or your body changing?

Do you have any concerns about fitting into the community?

THERAPIST/COUNSELLOR PERCEPTIONS

"One of the difficult things for transmen is you can be 23 and you start taking hormones and you look 13. So that can be a whole set of issues where age is very relevant and the question needs to be raised."

"First, coming out can happen at any age. The other thing is that older people are assumed not to have any sexuality whatsoever. They shouldn't even enjoy sex. When an older woman starts to talk about sexuality, she is often completely, totally dismissed, and yet that is such a big issue."

"I've encountered trans clients who feel uncomfortable with their sexuality. And they also feel uncomfortable with another person or a partner looking at their body. And are not sure that they will feel comfortable with a partner's body in a sexual situation."

B6

B7

HIV CONCERNS

HIV is a big concern for a lot of people. Can you tell me in what ways this may be true for you?

HIV AND AIDS
IS A CONCERN FOR ALL
LGBTTTIQ PEOPLE WHO ENGAGE IN HIGH-RISK SUBSTANCE USE OR SEXUAL PRACTICES.

RELEVANCE/INTENT

HIV and AIDS is a principal component in the lives of gay and bisexual men. Although more prevalent in the gay male community, HIV and AIDS is a concern for all LGBTTTIQ people who engage in high-risk substance use or sexual practices. Substance use and depression may increase clients' risk of acquiring HIV infection. However, substance use may also reduce fears around sexual behaviour and acquiring HIV infection.

Clients have concerns about preventing and treating HIV, HIV-testing and safer sexual practices. Therapists/counsellors need to assess clients' concerns or fears about the disease, as well as the impact it has had on them as members of LGBTTTIQ communities.

CLIENT PERCEPTIONS

"Drinking drove away my concerns about HIV. When I was feeling really down and depressed and at my worst with self-esteem and all that kind of stuff, getting drunk was a good way to throw all caution to the winds."

THERAPIST/COUNSELLOR PERCEPTIONS

"I'm thinking about the whole thing for a gay man around HIV and being affected by HIV, and lovers dying and friends dying, and living in a community that is dealing with this stress."

HIV and AIDS has had a major effect on LGBTTTIQ communities, especially gay and bixexual men. Most gay/bisexual men know someone who is HIV-positive and have lost partners or friends to AIDS. Therapists/counsellors should keep in mind the extreme grief and loss that HIV and AIDS has caused in the gay/bisexual male communities. HIV and AIDS has also had a big impact on the transgendered and transsexual communities, including increased transmission rates, particularly for transwomen. Many other LGBTTTIQ people, including lesbian and bixexual women, are actively involved in HIV/AIDS activism, or caring for friends with HIV/AIDS, and so they too may be impacted.

ADDITIONAL PROBES

Are there times when you thought a lot about or worried about HIV or AIDS?

Are you concerned about your own HIV status?

Are you concerned about a loved one's HIV status?

Has the AIDS epidemic had a personal impact on you?

THERAPIST/COUNSELLOR PERCEPTIONS

"Anyone who's suffering from low self-esteem or depression is not caring about themselves and are going to put themselves in high-risk situations. They aren't going to bother having safer sex, because they do not care."

"There are a lot of different issues. One of them is how does your sexual life go on after contracting HIV? How do you introduce condoms in the relationship?"

B7

B8

RELATIONSHIP BETWEEN SUBSTANCE USE AND/OR MENTAL HEALTH AND PART B ITEMS
Do you use alcohol and/or other drugs to cope with any of the issues we mentioned? Are your mental health concerns related to any of the issues we mentioned?
☐ not at all   ☐ a little   ☐ somewhat   ☐ a lot
If yes… in what ways?

THE RELATIONSHIP BETWEEN THE AFOREMENTIONED ISSUES AND CONCERNS ABOUT SUBSTANCE USE AND MENTAL HEALTH

CLIENT PERCEPTIONS

"For me, it was relevant to my using more because of the harassment I received for being gay, and just needing to wind down at times and to escape."

"I self-injure. I'm a cutter. As you can see, I am covered in scars. When I was young, I couldn't come out, so there was this whole secrecy thing. And so I'd cut because I was trying to express myself and let people know that I was hurting."

"I was 21 years old and went into a mental health facility due to an overdose of sleeping pills as a result of sexual abuse. As I was going through treatment, I realized I was also struggling with coming out. I found the mental health system beneficial in helping with that. I found it was a domino effect. Issues around coming out were impacting other aspects of my life."

RELEVANCE/INTENT

This item assesses the relationship between the aforementioned issues and substance use/mental health concerns, to find if the client uses substances to deal with these issues or if these issues are related to mental health problems.

Empirical and anecdotal evidence suggests that specific factors in the lives of LGBTTTIQ people are linked to substance use and/or mental health concerns. These factors include:
· having bars as the predominant social outlets
· finding friends in bars and falling into a heavy-using peer group
· developing an identity and "coming out" as LGBTTTIQ
· not accepting an LGBTTTIQ identity as a positive aspect of self
· carrying the burden of keeping up a secret identity
· being pathologized by the medical/psychological community
· experiencing racism, sexism, classism, ableism, heterosexism or genderism
· wanting to escape the restrictive sexual norms surrounding HIV infection
· losing family support
· lacking social support
· being denied housing, employment or appropriate health care
· being HIV-positive
· having a history of childhood adversity related to LGBTTTIQ identity
· experiencing trauma
· experiencing domestic violence (e.g., same-gender partner abuse).

ADDITIONAL PROBES

If so, under what circumstances?

When you were faced with the issues we just discussed (e.g., coming out to your family, feeling socially isolated), how did you cope?

B8

THERAPIST/COUNSELLOR PERCEPTIONS

"I ask about their coming-out process and look at potential links between drug and alcohol abuse onset or increases in that when they came out."

"I can't imagine how one would go through that journey of transitioning and coming out as trans without some kind of response, like depression, anxiety, panic attacks. They strike me as healthy responses to the insane culture that says 'Your body does not work. It's not right.'"

Counsellor competence

THIS GUIDE PROVIDES OPPORTUNITY AND CONTEXT
FOR FRAMING THE ASSESSMENT INTERVIEW.

CLIENT PERCEPTIONS

"My mother had just died and I started attending a bereavement support group. And I didn't come out to them about being trans because I didn't want it to influence the other members of the group's opinions of me, my experience as a part of a group, or my experience with the facilitators as part of a group. And then I started to realize that there was a tremendous number of things I couldn't address in a bereavement support group about what I was feeling about my mother's death. I couldn't talk about how the funeral was when I hadn't seen all these family members since before my transition. I couldn't talk to the facilitators of the group about what it was like to wonder whether or not my mother could accept me, never knowing now if she ultimately did."

"Being out and open about being gay, I don't have to tell any lies. I don't have to be secretive. I don't have to be part of a group that's exclusively straight and macho. I can be myself by being out."

We already conduct a lengthy assessment at our agency. Why is it necessary to add this extra piece?

Part A will only take a few minutes to be filled out by the client.

Sexual orientation and gender identity are basic information that therapists/counsellors need to know about clients to develop appropriate treatment/counselling plans. Sometimes, therapists/counsellors will make incorrect assumptions about a person's sexual orientation or gender identity. For example, they may assume a transsexual person is gay, or that a bisexual woman is a lesbian.

Clients might not volunteer information about their sexual orientation and gender identity at assessment or during counselling. Bisexual clients might only discuss their opposite-sex relationships. Transgendered clients might minimize their gender identity issues. Clients may not even necessarily disclose this information to LGBTTTIQ staff. They might assume staff members are straight.

During assessment, some LGBTTTIQ clients will look for indications that they can be open about their sexual orientation or gender identity during the treatment/counselling process. Some clients will wish to disclose this information, but may not have the opportunity. This guide provides this opportunity and the context for framing the assessment interview.

Will clients feel uncomfortable being asked about sexual orientation and gender identity at assessment?

Sexual orientation and gender identity may be sensitive issues for some clients. Other clients, however, may seek help specifically from LGBTTTIQ-positive service providers.

Some clients, especially those who have had negative experiences following self-disclosure of sexual orientation or gender identity, may not feel comfortable answering the items in Part A during an initial assessment. However, these items will let the client know that the therapist/counsellor or agency is aware of LGBTTTIQ identities. This may facilitate disclosure of sexual orientation and gender identity later during treatment/counselling.

When we field-tested the guide, participants reported that it was okay to discuss sexual orientation and gender identity issues during assessment. Some of the responses were:

"No problem answering the questions."

"Didn't bother me at all. The more they know about me, the better they can place me."

"I'm really open, so I am fine to discuss these things at any time."

"Good to get it out in the open so that you can discuss things. Sexual orientation and drug use are probably intermingled."

"Fine for me. Didn't mind being asked. I'm at a point where I am ready to talk about it."

"Made me think about things I wouldn't have considered much, so it was good in making me realize those things."

"It was fine, great to have a place to go where you don't have to hide your sexual orientation."

"Even though it's not my main concern, it was okay."

Therapists/counsellors who administered the guide during the field test made the following comments:

"I've used it and had a good response from clients. I feel it opened up dialogue."

"During the assessment, when I moved to this sheet, there was an immediate shift—the presence in the room—there was more comfort. It was more comfortable for the client and it was more comfortable for me."

"Clients were pleased to be asked. Some had never been asked before and they were struggling with their sexual orientation. No one was offended."

"I think this new assessment piece is really needed. I am glad to have this. I am sure we have missed a lot of clients who do not identify themselves as LGBTTTIQ at assessment. Unfortunately the assumption that everyone is straight is very prevalent."

THERAPIST/COUNSELLOR PERCEPTIONS

If someone doesn't feel safe enough to be honest with who they are, they are not going to feel safe enough or feel comfortable to address any issue, in terms of counselling. If that trust isn't there, it's a waste of their time to be coming to see you, because they're not really going to present their real situation and there's never going to be a good rapport, so therefore, there won't be a good working relationship."

"Before going into that whole section of questions, you should have a piece that is said to normalize things, like 'we recognize that there are lots of different sexual orientations, and sexual orientation can be fluid, and given that reality, we need to ask the following questions,' or something that sets the stage."

"You may have gone through family relationships, intimate relationships and social connections with the client, but they didn't disclose their sexual orientation or gender identity. Later, if they do disclose, those issues then need to be re-visited because there's a piece that wasn't discussed before that impacts on all those issues like family and intimacy. You didn't get the whole picture."

"I make sure clients know, 'We are not here to turn you into something. We're not here to corrupt you. We're not here to tell you that you are. You're the only one who knows who you are. You're the only one who'll have a choice in who you become. So, it's up to you.' Labels, when they're assigned by other people to us, become limited and limiting. When they're assigned to us by ourselves, they're empowering."

THERAPIST/COUNSELLOR PERCEPTIONS

"Changing our intake has had an impact on the numbers of clients who are identifying as LGBTTTIQ. Initially, when we started, we thought, well, what do we know? We know probably 10 per cent. Now, since we have implemented the ARQ questions, it's a 100 per cent increase. Now, our stats are telling us 20 per cent. It's probably more."

CLIENT PERCEPTIONS

"Some health professionals can be very biased and have really difficult attitudes. For example, there was one therapist that I was out to as a transwoman and I stopped seeing him simply because he tried putting words in my mouth. I said to him, 'I want children and I would love to have been able to have my own.' So, he sits up, looks at me and says, 'Oh, so you want to be a father, do you?' That immediately shut me right down. I lost trust in him."

What are the barriers to discussing sexual orientation and gender identity?
Many factors create barriers to discussing sexual orientation and gender identity. Therapists/counsellors often lack training, or believe:

· It is intrusive to ask.
· The client will be upset.
· Sexual orientation and gender identity are not relevant in treatment/counselling.

Staff and other clients, regardless of sexual orientation or gender identity, may lack understanding or have biased attitudes toward people whose sexual orientation or gender identity differs from their own.

Some staff may be concerned that clients will ask about the sexual orientation or gender identity of the therapist/counsellor. LGBTTTIQ staff working in predominantly heterosexual or mainstream settings may fear the professional consequences of self-disclosure. Therapists/counsellors of every sexual orientation and gender identity may be concerned about the impact of self-disclosure on the client or counselling relationship.

LGBTTTIQ clients may feel discomfort, anxiety or fear of negative consequences. They may fear being misunderstood by therapists/counsellors and other clients. Therapists/counsellors should remember that clients have probably had previous homophobic, transphobic or biphobic experiences in health or social service agencies.

I am only conducting the assessment and will not be involved in the treatment/counselling. Should I be asking about the client's sexual orientation and gender identity? Will this only "open up a can of worms" or bring up a lot of unrelated issues I won't have time to deal with?

Sexual orientation and gender identity, along with other topics that are considered sensitive, including domestic violence, child abuse, family substance use and use of mental health services, have a tremendous impact on clients. Basic information about these topics is necessary to develop appropriate treatment/counselling plans.

At assessment, you may not need to get deep into issues related to sexual orientation and gender identity. However, it is important to identify these issues and determine whether they need to be addressed during treatment/counselling. Clients struggling with their sexual orientation or gender identity will be reassured that they can discuss and be open about their concerns during treatment/counselling. When developing a treatment/counselling plan, the criteria you use (e.g., the Admission and Discharge criteria in Ontario) could indicate a particular level of service, but you may find that, locally, that service is not sensitive to LGBTTTIQ issues. This may mean you have to deviate from the criteria for the treatment/counselling plan and referrals.

The client's responses to Part A will help therapists/counsellors make the best referral possible.

Why discuss the issues in Part B?

The issues in Part B will help you:
· collect information to help formulate an appropriate treatment/ counselling plan
· maintain an effective relationship with clients by showing that you are aware of their issues.

CLIENT PERCEPTIONS

"My experiences were very much that the clinical staff and the nursing staff had just a tremendous amount of tolerance for other people hurling slurs at me. I think it's ignorance. I think it's lack of information and lack of training, but I also think that it's a really touchy subject for some. I think that a lot of people don't like conflict on that type of level. It's not that they think it's okay. They think it's a hard conversation to have with someone. In a clinical setting, someone might be afraid to stick up for the queer girl because they are afraid of how they will be perceived."

THERAPIST/COUNSELLOR PERCEPTIONS

"A few things will make it harder for a client to come out. Their assumptions about me as the therapist would make it harder. I think their initial interaction with me. I think the language I use. I mean, I'm pretty deliberate in saying, 'Do you have relationships with men or women?' That's not accidental. So, if I just ask my female clients about any relationships with men, it might make it harder for them to come out."

What can I do if I feel uncomfortable asking about sexual orientation and gender identity?

The following can help you become more comfortable:
· Educate yourself (see Resources).
· Become familiar with LGBTTTIQ resources in your area.
· Practice asking the questions in the guide.
· Role-play with a colleague.
· Consult with therapists/counsellors who have clinical experience in the area.
· Reflect on your own sexual orientation and gender identity to become more aware of feelings and biases that may help or inhibit discussion of sexual orientation and gender identity with clients. Deciding about whether to disclose your own orientation or identity to clients (if not already known) may be approached in the same way as deciding about sharing other personal information. Beyond your readiness or comfort in self-disclosing, would disclosure be helpful to the client and the counselling relationship, or might it have another effect? The client's needs should always take priority over other interests.

What can I do to help alleviate clients' concerns about discussing sexual orientation and gender identity?

Assess and counsel people in the context of their sexual orientation and gender identity. Be sensitive to (and reflect as appropriate) the language your client uses when referring to his or her identity and life.

When addressing transgendered or transsexual clients, use the proper pronouns based on their self-identity. When in doubt about the proper pronoun, it is fine to ask, "What is your preferred pronoun?" And then remember to use it. If you do slip up, apologize to the client and continue to use the preferred pronoun. For these clients, being seen as the gender that they are will greatly affect trust.

Increase your knowledge base, but avoid using clients as a primary source of your education about LGBTTTIQ people. Inviting additional information to better work with a client is appropriate; however, clients are there to receive your support, not to teach you.

Watch for unconscious bias or judgmental tendencies. Most of us have been socialized to "pathologize" LGBTTTIQ people.

Most of us are also raised to believe in binary thinking. Watch out for the "either/or" model of sexual orientation and the "either/or" model of gender identity—be careful not to push questioning clients to "choose."

Try to balance between the extremes of:
· assuming that being LGBTTTIQ is the underlying reason for substance use or mental health difficulties
· ignoring sexual orientation and gender identity altogether
· showing excessive curiosity about a client's identities.

Do not impose your values around if/when/where/how a client should come out. It is up to the client to consider what is involved in coming out.

Anti-LGBTTTIQ conversation or comments should not be tolerated in the treatment/counselling environment or client groups. Rather, therapists/counsellors should address these comments and create a culture of respect for diversity.

Ensure clients that all disclosed information will be kept confidential.

I am not LGBTTTIQ. How can I convey to a client that I am LGBTTTIQ-positive?

· Use this guide and create an atmosphere of acceptance. This can include placing LGBTTTIQ-positive posters, signs and reading materials in the agency or office. Offer appropriate support to clients who are exploring their sexual orientation or gender identity.
· Show that you accept the client's sexual orientation and gender identity, and make the client aware of any anti-discrimination policies at your agency/service.
· Keep a non-judgmental attitude and be aware of your body language.

CLIENT PERCEPTIONS

"If someone calls me by the wrong pronoun, I don't want to hear *why* they made the mistake. This has happened to me. They'll say, 'Oh, I'm sorry; it's because your brow ridge or your shoulders or your waist or your hips.' They'll tell you all the reasons why you don't pass. Shut up. I don't want to hear why I don't pass in their eyes or why any of us don't pass in their eyes. I just want to hear, 'I'm sorry.'"

"They didn't say, 'We're going to be sensitive to gender and sensitive to sexual orientation and sensitive to mental health.' If they had said those things, I might have known that I could expect support if others gave me a hard time. But because they just said, 'Oh yes, we want to be supportive and we want to be inclusive of everyone,' does that really mean that you are not going to think that I'm a freak?"

CLIENT PERCEPTIONS

"I think it is the institutional environment and attitudes towards these issues that are really important."

"Somehow, seeing rainbow flag stickers or queer-positive posters somewhere, those visual clues do make it more comfortable."

"When I found out about [an LGBTTTIQ-positive program], I was happy. I was ecstatic to learn of a program where I knew I wouldn't be judged. I could open up easily and get the help I needed."

"There should be one place where we will be able to go to deal with both the sexuality issues and the mental health issues because they relate to each other."

THERAPIST/COUNSELLOR PERCEPTIONS

"Obviously if internalized oppression is not dealt with, it can lead to death by suicide, or antisocial behaviour, or ongoing chronic mood disorders, like depression, sadness. There's no sunshine, no hope, no connection."

"When clients are dealing with a gender identity transition, it can be useful to know if their use of drugs or alcohol is connected to the huge stresses they are facing."

How can I/we make our practice or agency more LGBTTTIQ-positive?

POLICIES AND PROCEDURES
Take a look at your policies and procedures:
· Are they specific enough and inclusive of LGBTTTIQ people?
· Do they stipulate how you would handle discrimination from staff and clients?
· Do they communicate to staff the expected code of conduct?

CHANGE THE PHYSICAL SPACE
· Collect pamphlets, magazines, posters and newspapers from diverse communities to display in the waiting area.
· Consider unisex or gender-neutral bathrooms in your organization.

CREATE LGBTTTIQ-POSITIVE FORMS
· Questions that ask "Are you married" or limit gender to "M" and "F" have to go. Use this guide to create new forms.

CREATE LGBTTTIQ-SPECIFIC GROUPS
· LGBTTTIQ-specific groups help clients feel more comfortable discussing the issues discussed in this manual.

ADDRESSING DIFFERENCES AND BIASES IN GENERIC GROUPS
· Make groups safer for all marginalized groups, including LGBTTTIQ clients, by being "intentionally inclusive."
· Address differences in a very direct way.
· Use group guidelines and group norms that state that discriminatory remarks will not be tolerated in the group.
· Address and challenge discriminatory remarks as they arise during groups.

POSITIVE, TRAINED AND OUT STAFF
· Consider asking (and paying) local LGBTTTIQ groups to come to your organization to train your staff.
· Subscribe to journals and listservs that keep your staff up to date. See the list of references below for ideas.
· Recruit and hire LGBTTTIQ staff to work at your organization and encourage all staff to be LGBTTTIQ-positive.
· Ensure that human resources forms and practices are not genderist and heterosexist.

OUTREACH

· Create an outreach plan.
· Ensure your flyers indicate that LGBTTTIQ people are welcome and that your services reflect their needs.
· Make contact with LGBTTTIQ services and groups in your area. Is there a local paper, listserv, community bulletin board, bar or coffee shop where you could leave your flyers or otherwise spread the word?
· Ensure representation at LGBTTTIQ community events, such as Pride Day.

INPATIENT UNITS

· Be aware of the importance of chosen family for LGBTTTIQ clients. It may be important to keep visitor guidelines as flexible as possible.
· Respect the importance of LGBTTTIQ books and pictures. Allow clients to make their surroundings more familiar and comfortable.
· Address differences in a very direct way.
· Address and challenge discriminatory remarks as they arise on the unit.

LGBTTTIQ REPRESENTATION AND DECISION MAKING

Ensure that LGBTTTIQ staff and community members are involved in:
· your hiring committees
· strategic planning
· your board or advisory committees.

THERAPIST/COUNSELLOR PERCEPTIONS

"Is it okay to talk about sex with a psychiatric patient? Well, not really. It's awkward. It's embarrassing. And do they actually have a right to a sexual drive in a psychiatric ward locked up somewhere? And who wants to acknowledge that? That's very challenging. It makes things more complicated. But the reality is, those people experience homophobia as well. It's important. But is it more complicated to work with that? Yes, it's more complicated."

CLIENT PERCEPTIONS

"There's all of that internalized oppression within the 'crazy' community too, where, 'She's crazier than I am therefore, she's lower on the totem pole.' Or, 'I'm only depressed; she's schizophrenic.' There's so much of that. 'I'm only schizophrenic; she's schizophrenic and gay.' And then you go lower and lower. 'She's schizophrenic, gay and black.' This multiple piling on of marginalizations, and you get lower and lower."

THERAPIST/COUNSELLOR PERCEPTIONS

"There is a huge stigma associated with coming out in the black community. So I rarely get black clients who identify as LGBTTTIQ, although I do have clients who are black. And what that often means is they don't feel they can access culture-specific programs, especially within the LGBTTTIQ communities, because there's a possibility that there will be somebody there who knows the family or whatever."

"I have one client who is a refugee claimant and he's gay. When a person presents with those multiple layers—the cultural thing, the religious thing and sexual orientation—it takes on a different degree and intensity, because of all of those layers of isolation and estrangement."

What are some of the specific needs, concerns and/or experiences of LGBTTTIQ people of colour or other queer people from marginalized communities?

Coming out and finding support is harder for people who are doubly or triply marginalized.

For example, a deaf lesbian may experience discrimination from the deaf community around her sexual orientation and discrimination around her disability from the LGBTTTIQ communities. She may not find appropriate supports from either the LGBTTTIQ services or agencies for deaf people. She may need to develop connections in a deaf LGBTTTIQ community. This unique type of support is available in large cities, but it may not exist in other places. The Internet may be one resource for people looking to meet others with similar experiences.

LGBTTTIQ people of colour often face a similar double marginalization—it may be challenging to be "all of who they are" in the various LGBTTTIQ and racial communities to which they belong. LGBTTTIQ people of colour experience racism from a predominantly white queer community. However, the ethnospecific communities from which they originate may have been places of support and shelter from racism in general society. Coming out carries the risk of losing this important support.

When working with LGBTTTIQ people who belong to marginalized communities (other than the LGBTTTIQ community), clinicians need to be aware of the additional challenges and should ask clients about this experience.

Where possible, provide a list of groups and services specifically for LGBTTTIQ people of colour, LGBTTTIQ people with disabilities and LGBTTTIQ people from other marginalized communities.

Can the questions in the ARQ2 guide be used with clients who have severe mental health problems?

Sexual orientation and gender identity are basic information that therapists/counsellors need to know about all clients. Often, people with severe mental illness (e.g., schizophrenia, psychosis) must cope with having their sexual orientation and gender identity go unrecognized. Faulty assumptions are often made that these people are not sexual.

A prevailing social myth is that people become lesbian or gay because "something bad" happened to them, such as the idea that sexual abuse "caused" their sexual orientation. Counsellors/therapists working with survivors of childhood sexual abuse will need to be aware of this myth and help the client expose and debunk the myth as part of their healing work. For example, it is helpful for a client to hear a clinician say, "There is no correlation between the abuse and your sexual orientation."

In emergency and crisis situations, we recommend that clinicians use their best judgment in deciding when, how and if the ARQ2 guide is to be used. Clinicians should consider that in some crisis situations, sensitive questions regarding sexual orientation and gender identity might help the clinician and the client to better understand and resolve the causes of the crisis. For example, an LGBTTTIQ person who is coming out or transitioning may present to an emergency department with suicidality after being rejected by a family member.

CLIENT PERCEPTIONS

"I had a nervous breakdown and I told this girl on the ward that, 'If they tell you I'm gay, don't believe them.' That just started an uproar. I thought eventually that they were trying to kill me. It was horrible. I was having these delusions and hearing voices that they were coming for me, and it's a very scary experience. It was mostly fabricated in my head, because of the symptoms I was having. But because of the homophobia and abuse that I have had to deal with, it makes it even scarier and more threatening."

"I came out to my psychiatrist. He says, 'It's good to be a lesbian. Just don't have sex with women.' I had abuse issues with my mother and he thinks if I have sex with women, it will trigger. Many, many, many straight women are abused by men. So, is the advice, 'You shouldn't have sex with men because it will trigger'?"

Resources:

Internet sites

THERAPIST/COUNSELLOR PERCEPTIONS

"One of the hardest issues I have is trying to find recreational leisure activities in the gay community that are completely abstinent from drugs and alcohol.... So when I'm referring someone to a club or an activity, I am thinking, 'Boy, I know this is a club that they could be potentially triggered by,' so I sometimes will caution them about exploring it, but to at least give it a try rather than become isolated."

"Some religious communities are affirming and you can still practice your faith. I find it's very important to help clients find a safe space, or an organization of Jewish lesbians, or an organization of people from the Caribbean who are practicing and open or whatever the case may be."

Diversity within LGBTTTIQ communities

The Internet is a useful resource for information about LGBTTTIQ people of colour or other queer people from marginalized communities. The following are examples of Internet sites representing the diversity of the community (not an exhaustive list):

www.trikone.org
(Queer people of South Asian heritage)

www.acas.org
(Asian Community AIDS Service)

www.the519.org/programs/groups/queer/hola.shtml
(Gay Latinos)

www.geocities.com/orad_ca
(Ontario Rainbow Alliance of the Deaf)

www.legit.ca
(Lesbian and Gay Immigration Task Force)

http://bi.org/db/dis.html
(Resources for bisexual people living with disabilities)

www.2spirits.com
(Two-Spirited People of the First Nations)

www.pinktriangle.org
(Ottawa GLBT Seniors)

www.salaamcanada.com
(Queer Muslims)

General information about LGBTTTIQ communities

www.qrd.org/qrd/www/orgs/aja/lgbt.htm
(L/G/B/Ts on the WWW)

www.thetaskforce.org
(National Gay and Lesbian Task Force, United States)

www.isna.org
(Intersex Society of North America)

www.torontobinet.org
(Toronto Bisexual Network)

www.the519.org/programs/trans/ON_TS_ResourceGuide.htm
(info on resources for transpeople across Ontario)

Addiction/mental health information

www.lgtbcentrevancouver.com/pdf_s/theManual_vFinal.pdf
(LGBT Health Matters manual)

www.vch.ca/ce/docs/03_02_LGBTSubstanceUse.pdf
(LGBT Communities and Substance Abuse—What Health Has to Do
With It! report)

www.ccsa.ca/CCSA/EN/Topics/Populations/LGBTTTIQ.htm
(Canadian Centre on Substance Abuse's LGBTTTIQ page)

www.nalgap.org
(National Association of Gay & Lesbian Addiction Professionals)

www.health.org
(U.S. Department of Health & Human Services and SAMHSA's
National Clearinghouse for Alcohol & Drug Information)

www.trans-health.com
(Online Magazine of Health and Fitness for Transsexual and
Transgendered People)

hsl.mcmaster.ca/tomflem/gayprob.html
(Health care information and resources)

www.bbcm.org
(Bad Boy Club Montreal)

www.womenfdn.org/resources/info/pdfs/lesbian.pdf
(The Women's Addiction Foundation's document: Lesbian and
Bisexual Women and Substance Use)

www.sherbourne.on.ca/programs/programs.html
(Sherbourne Health Centre's links page)

www.caps.ucsf.edu/TRANS/TRANScriticalneeds.pdf
(Critical Health Needs of MtF Transgenders of Colour report)

THERAPIST/COUNSELLOR PERCEPTIONS

"Identity is very important. When you don't
have a sense of identity, it affects mental
health. I think that there are two issues.
One, how do being queer, realizing you are
queer, coming out and sexual orientation
issues affect mental health? And two,
you may already have come out and then
developed mental health issues, and in
that case, the issue is how to access
appropriate services. I definitely think
that being queer is a risk factor, just like
any oppression."

"Having a trans identity means you have
a mental health disorder, according to the
current DSM. So, being trans is a mental
health issue, and so HIV, body image,
dating, the bar scene, everything in ARQ,
plays a huge role in how transpeople view
themselves, how they are viewed by other
people, how they feel about themselves,
how they feel in society."

"For gay men, body image is very important.
Eating disorders are going up in young
men. Everything hinges on how they look.
There is pressure to be young and attractive.
For someone coming out and not perfect,
there are feelings of isolation and self-
esteem issues."

THERAPIST/COUNSELLOR PERCEPTIONS

"[The issues include] victimization or surviving in victim mode as a result of constant heterosexism, having to live in a heterosexist environment and the damage that's done to the soul, the identity, the self-esteem, relationships, all of that."

"People's support networks are often different, and what people consider the family structure is different, as well as what kinds of ties exist between the family of origin. I think it's a lot more common that people are cut off from their families of origin. And so that support may not be there for them."

"I think it's important to provide your family when you're coming out with some kind of support or resource, whether it's somebody that they can talk to, a book that they can read, or a video they can watch."

Information on discrimination

www.egale.ca
(EGALE Canada)

www.ncf.ca/gay/police-gay
(Ottawa Police Gay and Lesbian Liaison Committee)

www.srlp.org
(Sylvia Rivera Law Project)

www.hrusa.org
(Human Rights Resource Center, University of Minnesota)

www.actwin.com/cahp
(Citizens Against Homophobia)

Information on family issues

www.colage.org
(Children of Gays and Lesbians Everywhere)

www.uwo.ca/pridelib/family
(Family Pride Canada)

www.fsatoronto.com/programs/fsaprograms/davekelley/
lgbtparenting.html
(LGBT Parenting Network)

http://naples.cc.sunysb.edu/CAS/affirm.nsf
(Psychologists Affirming their Gay, Lesbian & Bisexual Family)

www.rainbowhealth.ca/english/index.html
(Canadian Rainbow Health Coalition)

Resources:

Bibliography

Barbara, A.M. (2002). Issues in substance abuse treatment with lesbian, gay and bisexual people: A qualitative analysis of service providers. *Journal of Gay & Lesbian Social Services, 14,* 1–17.

Center for Substance Abuse Prevention (CSAP). (2000). *Substance abuse resource guide: Lesbian, gay, bisexual and transgendered populations.* Rockville, MD: CSAP.

Center for Substance Abuse Treatment. (CSAT). (2001). *A provider's introduction to substance abuse treatment for lesbian, gay, bisexual and transgendered individuals.* Rockville, MD: CSAT.

Coalition for Lesbian & Gay Rights in Ontario/Project Affirmation. (1997). *Systems failure: A report on the experiences of sexual minorities in Ontario's health-care and social-services system.* Toronto: Health Canada.

Crisp, C. (2006). The gay affirmative practice scale (GAP): A new measure for assessing cultural competence with gay and lesbian clients. *Social Work, 51* (2), 115–126.

Dallas, D. (1998). *Current concepts in transgender identity.* New York: Garland Press.

DeBord, K.A. & Perez, R.M. (2000). Group counselling theory and practice with lesbian, gay, and bisexual clients. In Perez, R.M., DeBord, K.A. & Bieschke, K.J. (Eds.), *Handbook of counselling and psychotherapy with lesbian, gay and bisexual clients* (pp. 183–206). Washington: American Psychological Association.

Docter, R.F. (1990). *Transvestites and transsexuals: Towards a theory of cross-gender behavior.* New York: Plenum Press.

Doctor, F. (in press). The Rainbow Women's Group: Reflections on group work with lesbian, bi and transwomen who have drug and alcohol concerns. In N. Poole & L. Greaves (Eds.), *Women and Substance Use: Current Canadian Perspectives.* Toronto: Centre for Addiction and Mental Health.

Doctor, F. (2003). Examining links between drug and alcohol use and experiences of homophobia/biphobia and coming out. In J. Whitman & C. Boyd (Eds.), *The Therapist's Notebook for Lesbian, Gay and Bisexual Clients* (pp. 262–267). New York: Haworth Clinical Practice Press.

Doctor, F. (2004). Working with lesbian, gay, bisexual, transsexual, transgender, two-spirit, intersex and queer (LGBTTTIQ) people who have substance use concerns. In S. Harrison & V. Carver (Eds.), *Alcohol and Drug Problems: A Practical Guide for Counsellors* (3rd ed.) (pp. 353–382). Toronto: Centre for Addiction and Mental Health.

Eliason, M.J. (1996). *Who cares? Institutional barriers to health care for lesbian, gay, and bisexual people.* New York: National League for Nursing Press.

Feinberg, L. (2001). Trans health crisis: For us it's life or death. *American Journal of Public Health, 91* (6), 897–900.

Garnets, L.D. & Kimmel, D.C. (Eds.). (1993). *Psychological perspectives of lesbians and gay male experiences.* New York: Columbia University Press.

Gay and Lesbian Medical Association. (2002). *Creating a safe clinical environment for lesbian, gay, bisexual, transgender and intersex (LGBTI) patients* [On-line]. Available: www.glma.org.

Gay and Lesbian Medical Association. (2002). *MSM: Clinician guide to incorporating sexual risk assessment in routine visits* [On-line]. Available: www.glma.org.

Greene, B. (Ed.). (1994). *Women of color: Integrating ethnic and gender identities in psychotherapy.* Newbury Park, CA: Sage.

Greene, B. (Ed.). (1997). *Ethnic and cultural diversity among lesbians and gay men.* Newbury Park, CA: Sage.

Guss, J.R. & Drescher, J. (Eds.). (2000). *Addictions in the gay and lesbian community.* Binghamton, NY: Haworth Press.

Israel, G.E & Tarver, D.E. (1997). *Transgender care: Recommended guidelines, practical information, and personal accounts.* Philadelphia, PA: Temple University Press.

Jones, B.E. & Hill, M.J. (2002). *Mental health issues in lesbian, gay, bisexual, and transgender communities.* Washington, DC: American Psychiatric Publishing.

Kessler, S. (1998). *Lessons from the intersexed.* Piscataway, NJ: Rutgers University Press.

Kettelhack, G. (1999). *Vastly more than that.* Center City, MN: Hazelden.

Kominars, S.B. & Kominars, K.D. (1996). *Accepting ourselves and others: A journal in recovery from addictive and compulsive behavior for gays, lesbians, bisexuals and their therapists.* Center City, MN: Hazelden.

Kus, R.J. (1985). Stages of coming out: An ethnographic approach. *Western Journal of Nursing Research, 7,* 177–198.

Kus, R.J. (1995). *Addiction and recovery in gay and lesbian persons.* New York: Harrington Park Press.

Longres, J.F. (Ed.). (1996). *Men of color: A context for service to homo-sexually active men.* New York: Park Press.

MacEwan, I. & Kinder, P. (1991). *Making visible: Improving services for lesbians and gay men in alcohol and drug treatment health promotion.* Wellington, New Zealand: Alcoholic Liquor Advisory Council.

Moore, L.C. (1989). *Does your mama know? An anthology of Black lesbian coming out stories.* Decatur, GA: Red Bone Press.

Ochs, R. (Ed). (2001). *The Bisexual Resource Guide 2001* (4th ed.). Cambridge, MA: Bisexual Resource Centre.

Oggins, J. & Eichenbaum, J. (2002). Engaging transgender substance users in substance use treatment. *International Journal of Transgenderism, 6* (2) [On-line]. Available: www.symposion.com/ijt/ijtvo06no02_03.htm. Accessed: September 26, 2006.

Perez, R.M., DeBord, K.A. & Bieschke, K.J. (Eds.) (2000). *Handbook of counselling and psychotherapy with lesbian, gay and bisexual clients.* Washington, DC: American Psychological Association.

Raj, R. (2002). Towards a transpositive therapeutic model: Developing clinical sensitivity and cultural competence in the effective support of transsexual and transgendered clients. *The International Journal of Transgenderism, 6* [On-line]. Available: http://www.symposion.com/ijt/ijtvo06no02_04.htm.

Schneider, M.S. (Ed.). (1997). *Pride & prejudice: Working with lesbian, gay and bisexual youth.* Toronto: Central Toronto Youth Services.

Simpson, B. (1994). *Making substance use and other services more accessible to lesbian, gay and bisexual youth.* Toronto: Central Toronto Youth Services.

Trans Programming at the 519. (no date). *TS/TG 101: An introduction to transsexual and transgendered issues for service providers.* Toronto: The 519 Community Centre [On-line]. Available: http://www.the519.org/.

Transgender Protocol Team. (Ed.). (1995). *Transgender protocol: Treatment services guidelines for substance abuse treatment providers.* San Francisco: Lesbian, Gay, Bisexual, Transgender Substance Abuse Task Force.

van der Meide, W. (2001). *The intersection of sexual orientation and race: Considering the experiences of lesbian, gay, bisexual, transgendered ("LGBT") people of colour & two-spirited people.* Ottawa: EGALE Canada.

Van Wormer, K., Wells, J. & Boes, M. (2000). *Social work with lesbians, gays and bisexuals.* Toronto: Allyn and Bacon.

Weinberg, M., Williams, S. & Pryor, D. (1994). *Dual attraction: Understanding bisexuality.* New York: Oxford University Press.

Weinberg, T.S. (1994). *Gay men, drinking, and alcoholism.* Carbondale, IL: Southern Illinois Press.

Weinstein, D.L. (1992). *Lesbians and gay men: Chemical dependency treatment issues.* New York: Harrington Park Press.

Whitman, J.S. & Boyd, C.J. (2003). *The therapist's notebook for lesbian, gay, and bisexual clients: Homework, handouts, and activities for use in psychotherapy.* New York: Haworth Clinical Practice Press.

Resources:

Glossary

Changes in thinking and attitudes toward sexual orientation and gender identity are continually taking place in society as a whole and within the LGBTTTIQ communities. **THE DISCOURSE AROUND LGBTTTIQ ISSUES AND THE DEFINITIONS IN THIS GLOSSARY WILL CHANGE OVER TIME.** These terms and definitions are not standardized and may be used differently by different people and in different regions.

ASEXUAL: a word describing a person who is not sexually and/or romantically active, or not sexually and/or romantically attracted to other persons.

AUTOSEXUAL: a word describing a person whose significant sexual involvement is with oneself or a person who prefers masturbation to sex with a partner.

BIPHOBIA: irrational fear or dislike of bisexuals. Bisexuals may be stigmatized by heterosexuals, lesbians and gay men.

BI-POSITIVE: the opposite of biphobia. A bi-positive attitude is one that validates, affirms, accepts, appreciates, celebrates and integrates bisexual people as unique and special in their own right.

BISEXUAL: a word describing a person whose sexual orientation is directed toward men and women, though not necessarily at the same time.

COMING OUT: the process by which LGBTTTIQ people acknowledge and disclose their sexual orientation or gender identity, or in which transsexual or transgendered people acknowledge and disclose their gender identity, to themselves and others (See also "Transition"). Coming out is thought to be an ongoing process. People who are "closeted" or "in the closet" hide the fact that they are LGBTTTIQ. Some people "come out of the closet" in some situations (e.g., with other gay friends) and not in others (e.g., at work).

CROSSDRESSER: A person who dresses in the clothing of the other sex for recreation, expression or art, or for erotic gratification. Formerly known as "transvestites." Crossdressers may be male or female, and can be straight, gay, lesbian or bisexual. Gay/bisexual male cross-dressers may be "drag queens" or female impersonators; lesbian/bisexual female crossdressers may be "drag kings" or male impersonators.

DYKE: a word traditionally used as a derogatory term for lesbians. Other terms include lezzie, lesbo, butch, bull dyke and diesel dyke. Many women have reclaimed these words and use them proudly to describe their identity.

FAG: a word traditionally used as a derogatory term for gay men. Other terms include fruit, faggot, queen, fairy, pansy, sissy and homo. Many men have reclaimed these words and use them proudly to describe their identity.

FAMILY OF CHOICE: the circle of friends, partners, companions and perhaps ex-partners with which many LGBTTTIQ people surround themselves. This group gives the support, validation and sense of belonging that is often unavailable from the person's family of origin.

FAMILY OF ORIGIN: the biological family or the family that was significant in a person's early development.

GAY: a word to describe a person whose primary sexual orientation is to members of the same gender or who identifies as a member of the gay community. This word can refer to men and women, although many women prefer the term "lesbian."

GAY-POSITIVE: the opposite of homophobia. A gay-positive attitude is one that affirms, accepts, appreciates, celebrates and integrates gay and lesbian people as unique and special in their own right.

GENDER CONFORMING: abiding by society's gender rules, e.g., a woman dressing, acting, relating to others and thinking of herself as feminine or as a woman.

GENDER IDENTITY: a person's own identification of being male, female or intersex; masculine, feminine, transgendered or transsexual. Gender identity most often corresponds with one's anatomical gender, but sometimes people's gender identity doesn't directly correspond to their anatomy. Transgendered people use many terms to describe their gender identities, including: pre-op transsexual, post-op transsexual, non-op transsexual, transgenderist, crossdresser, transvestite, transgendered, two-spirit, intersex, hermaphrodite, fem male, gender blender, butch, manly woman, diesel dyke, sex radical, androgynist, female impersonator, male impersonator, drag king, drag queen, etc.

GENDERQUEER: this very recent term was coined by young people who experience a very fluid sense of both their gender identity and their sexual orientation, and who do not want to be constrained by absolute or static concepts. Instead, they prefer to be open to relocate themselves on the gender and sexual orientation continuums.

GENDER ROLE: the public expression of gender identity. Gender role includes everything people do to show the world they are male, female, androgynous or ambivalent. It includes sexual signals, dress, hairstyle and manner of walking. In society, gender roles are usually considered to be masculine for men and feminine for woman.

GENDER TRANSITION: the period during which transsexual persons begin changing their appearance and bodies to match their internal identity.

GENDERISM: the belief that the binary construct of gender, in which there are only two genders (male and female), is the most normal, natural and preferred gender identity. This binary construct does not include or allow for people to be intersex, transgendered, transsexual or genderqueer.

HATE CRIMES: offences that are motivated by hatred against victims based on their actual or perceived race, color, religion, national origin, ethnicity, gender, disability or sexual orientation.

HETEROSEXISM: the assumption, expressed overtly and/or covertly, that all people are or should be heterosexual. Heterosexism excludes the needs, concerns, and life experiences of lesbian, gay and bisexual people, while it gives advantages to heterosexual people. It is often a subtle form of oppression that reinforces silence and invisibility for lesbian, gay and bisexual people.

HETEROSEXUAL: term used to describe a person who primary sexual orientation is to members of the opposite gender. Heterosexual people are often referred to as "straight."

HETEROSEXUAL PRIVILEGE: the unrecognized and assumed privileges that people have if they are heterosexual. Examples of heterosexual privilege include: holding hands or kissing in public without fearing threat, not questioning the normalcy of your sexual orientation, raising children without fears of state intervention or worries that your children will experience discrimination because of your heterosexuality.

HOMOPHOBIA: irrational fear, hatred, prejudice or negative attitudes toward homosexuality and people who are gay or lesbian. Homophobia can take overt and covert, as well as subtle and extreme, forms. Homophobia includes behaviours such as jokes, name-calling, exclusion, gay bashing, etc.

HOMOSEXUAL: a term to describe a person whose primary sexual orientation is to members of the same gender. Most people prefer to not use this label, preferring to use other terms, such as gay or lesbian.

IDENTITY: how one thinks of oneself, as opposed to what others observe or think about one.

INTERNALIZED HOMOPHOBIA: fear and self-hatred of one's own sexual orientation that occurs for many lesbians and gay men as a result of heterosexism and homophobia. Once lesbians and gay men realize that they belong to a group of people that is often despised and rejected in our society, many internalize and incorporate this stigmatization, and fear or hate themselves.

INTERSEX: a person who has some mixture of male and female genetic and/or physical sex characteristics. Formerly called "hermaphrodites." Many intersex people consider themselves to be part of the trans community.

LESBIAN: a female whose primary sexual orientation is to other women or who identifies as a member of the lesbian community.

LGBTTTIQ: a common acronym for lesbian, gay, bisexual, transsexual, transgendered, two-spirit, intersex and queer individuals/communities. This acronym may or may not be used in a particular community. For example, in some places, the acronym LGBT (for lesbian, gay, bisexual and transgendered/transsexual) may be more common.

MSM: refers to any man who has sex with a man, whether he identifies as gay, bisexual or heterosexual. This term highlights the distinction between sexual behaviour and sexual identity (i.e., sexual orientation). A person's sexual behaviour may manifest itself into a sexual identity, but the reverse is not always true; sexual orientation is not always reflective of sexual behaviour. For example, a man may call himself heterosexual, but may engage in sex with men in certain situations (e.g., prison, sex work).

OUT OR OUT OF THE CLOSET: varying degrees of being open about one's sexual orientation or gender identity.

PASSING: describes transgendered or transsexual people's ability to be accepted as their preferred gender. The term refers primarily to acceptance by people the individual does not know, or who do not know that the individual is transgendered or transsexual. Typically, passing involves a mix of physical gender cues (e.g., clothing, hairstyle, voice), behaviour, manner and conduct when interacting with others. Passing can also refer to hiding one's sexual orientation, as in "passing for straight."

POLYSEXUAL: an orientation that does not limit affection, romance or sexual attraction to any one gender or sex, and that further recognizes there are more than just two sexes.

QUEER: traditionally, a derogatory and offensive term for LGBTTTIQ people. Many LGBTTTIQ people have reclaimed this word and use it proudly to describe their identity. Some transsexual and transgendered people identify as queers; others do not.

QUESTIONING: people who are questioning their gender identity or sexual orientation and who often choose to explore options.

SEXUAL BEHAVIOUR: what people do sexually. Not necessarily congruent with sexual orientation and/or sexual identity.

SEXUAL IDENTITY: one's identification to self (and others) of one's sexual orientation. Not necessarily congruent with sexual orientation and/or sexual behaviour.

SEXUAL MINORITIES: include people who identify as LGBTTTIQ.

SEXUAL ORIENTATION: a term for the emotional, physical, romantic, sexual and spiritual attraction, desire or affection for another person. Examples include heterosexuality, bisexuality and homosexuality.

SIGNIFICANT OTHER: a life partner, domestic partner, lover, boyfriend or girlfriend. It is often equivalent to the term "spouse" for LGBTTTIQ people.

STRAIGHT: a term often used to describe people who are heterosexual.

TRANS and **TRANSPEOPLE** are non-clincial terms that usually include transsexual, transgendered and other gender-variant people.

TRANSGENDERED: a person whose gender identity is different from his or her biological sex, regardless of the status of surgical and hormonal gender reassignment processes. Often used as an umbrella term to include transsexuals, transgenderists, transvestites (crossdressers), and two-spirit, intersex and transgendered people.

TRANSGENDERIST: someone who is in-between being a transsexual and a transgendered person on the gender continuum, and who often takes sex hormones, but does not want genital surgery. Transgenderists can be born male (formerly known as "she-males") or born females (one called he/shes"). The former sometimes obtain breast implants and/or electrolysis.

TRANSITION: the process (which for some people may also be referred to as the "gender reassignment process") whereby transsexual people change their appearance and bodies to match their internal (gender) identity, while living their lives full-time in their preferred gender role.

TRANSPHOBIA: irrational fear or dislike of transsexual and transgendered people.

TRANSPOSITIVE: the opposite of transphobia. A transpositive attitude is one that validates, affirms, accepts, appreciates, celebrates and integrates transsexual and transgendered people as unique and special in their own right.

TRANSSENSUAL: a term for a person who is primarily attracted to trans-gendered or transsexual people.

TRANSSEXUAL: a term for a person who has an intense long-term experience of being the sex opposite to his or her birth-assigned sex and who typically pursues a medical and legal transformation to become the other sex. There are transmen (female-to-male transsexuals) and trans-women (male-to-female transsexuals). Transsexual people may undergo a number of procedures to bring their body and public identity in line with their self-image, including sex hormone therapy, electrolysis treatments, sex reassignment surgeries and legal changes of name and sex status.

References

Cass, V.C. (1979). Homosexual identity formation: A theoretical model. *Journal of Homosexuality, 4,* 219–235.

Devor, H. (1997). *FTM: Female-to-male transsexuals in society.* Bloomington, IN: Indiana University Press.

Harmer, J. (2000). *Older gay, bisexual, transgender, transsexual persons; Community services challenges and opportunities for the 519 Community Centre and the GLBT community, A review.* Toronto: The 519 Community Centre [On-line]. Available: www.the519.org/public_html/programs/older/index.shtml.

Meyer, I.H. (2003). Prejudice, social stress, and mental health in lesbian, gay, and bisexual populations: Conceptual issues and research evidence. *Psychological Bulletin, 129,* 674–697.

Appendix: Creating the Guide and Manual

The content for this manual was developed through two phases of the project:

Phase 1: ARQ—Addictions

We conducted focus groups, individual in-person interviews and telephone interviews with 26 clinicians from Ontario (Toronto, Ottawa and London) who had clinical experience working with LGBTTTIQ clients with substance use problems. We collected data about the content and process of assessment and the issues specific to these clients.

We also conducted focus groups and individual interviews with 38 past and current clients of the LesBiGay Service (now Rainbow Services) at the Centre for Addiction and Mental Health (CAMH). Most of the clients identified as gay or lesbian, and a small percentage identified as bisexual. As there were very few transgendered or transsexual clients in the LesBiGay Service at that time, they were not included in this phase of the study. Data we collected included information about the content and process of assessment, disclosure of sexual orientation in addiction services and the issues specific to LGBTTTIQ clients with substance use problems.

We then used the results of the focus groups and interviews to develop a template of the guide. This template was field-tested with clinicians from the Assessment and LesBiGay Services at CAMH and was reviewed by external clinicians.

Finally, we asked for satisfaction responses from clients who were administered the new template.

In addition, because we were unable to reach clients from diverse populations, we sought information from secondary resources and from people in diverse communities for their added comments.

Phase 2: ARQ2—Mental Health, Counselling and Addictions

In this phase of the project, we conducted focus groups, individual in-person interviews and telephone interviews with 29 service providers from Ontario (Toronto, Ottawa, London, Sudbury, Sault Ste. Marie) and British Columbia (Vancouver, Fort Nelson) who had clinical experience working with LGBTTTIQ clients with mental health problems. We collected data about the issues specific to these clients. Service providers were also asked to identify any gaps in the original ARQ manual, especially those related to mental health.

We conducted focus groups and individual interviews with 31 people who had used mental health services in Ontario. Participants identified as gay (14), lesbian/dyke (9), bisexual (4), queer (3), two-spirit (1), MSM (1) or WSW (1). Six participants identified as transsexual or transgendered. The most common mental health concerns were depression and anxiety. Others included bipolar disorder, trauma, suicidality, schizoaffective disorder, borderline personality disorder, Asperger's syndrome, self-harm, seasonal affective disorder and obsessive-compulsive disorder. We collected data about disclosure of sexual orientation and gender identity in mental health services and the issues specific to LGBTTTIQ clients with mental health concerns.

The results of the focus groups and interviews were analyzed and used to revise the manual.

Finally, we asked service providers working in the community (at other agencies or in private practice) to review the revised manual for further comments.